A St ... **... ....**

Written by Gordon McClure

Illustrated by Shaun McClure

Edited by Katie Hatfield

Across the fields of yesterday
He sometimes comes to me;
A little lad just back from play -
The lad I used to be.

And yet he smiles so wistfully
Once he has crept within,
I wonder if he hopes to see
The man I might have been.

Thomas S. Jones

This book is dedicated to my sons, family and friends;
without whom, these stories would not be possible, as their
lives were intertwined in the telling.

Contents

A Stirring of Echoes

I was born in Wythenshawe, Manchester, on the 14th February, 1948, in my Grandparents' council house on Lawton Moor Road. The first of eight children born to Sheena and William (Bill) McClure.

I am told that there were some complications with my birth and I entered the world a strange blue hue. This startled my Grandmother as there was no midwife present which caused her to speculate on who the Father was. After all, her son, Bill, was not blue. He was definitely white!

Help arrived, along with saner heads, and it was explained to my Grandmother that my strange colour was due to a lack of oxygen and after they got my circulation going again, all would be well, and I would morph into a baby whose pigmentation would be more in-line with that of his parents. My Grandmother was mightily relieved! I suspect she was more relieved about the parental issue being resolved than she was about my well-being, but maybe I am being harsh.

Just as peace descended, punctuated only by the occasional cry of protest from myself, the calm was shattered by the sound of a trumpet playing. My Dad, hit by a wave of sentiment on hearing the cries heralding my birth, took it upon himself to sit on the stairs and give us a rendering of *My Funny Valentine*. (I was born on Saint Valentine's day.)

The midwife must have thought that she was in a mad house. I was beginning to harbour the same thoughts myself!

(The funny thing is, I grew up liking certain types of jazz and my favourite colour is blue.)

*****

My parents met during the War. My Father was in the RAF and my Mother was in the WRAF (the female equivalent). They were stationed at the same camp. Dad was a corporal whose job it was to repair damaged aircraft. Mum was from Inverness, Scotland, whose job it was to cause trouble.

For reasons never explained, Dad was given the job of trying to bring all of the camps' troublemakers, misfits and general arseholes back into line. He had no training in this, and I can only conclude that the Air Force had it in for him to burden him with such a task. It was whilst performing these duties that he met my Mother. She came under the 'troublemaker' category. Sometime later, they were married in the Manchester Registry Office.

After the War, my parents moved in with my Grandparents in Manchester. My Gran was something of a 'Hyacinth Bucket' type character. She would put on a posh voice when dealing with doctors and the like...but she was everything a Gran should be: plump; jolly; kind-hearted; and smelled of talc and lavender. Grandad showed little interest in any of his Grandchildren. My memory of him is of a handsome, slim man, who just sat in his chair all day smoking his pipe. Of course, I only got to really know him through our occasional trips over the Pennines from Yorkshire and, by that time, he was retired. He wasn't nasty to us or anything like that, but you could not engage him in conversation.

In the sixties, they decided to do away with their coal fire and purchase an electric one. They chose a 'Magicoal' electric fire; these were popular at the time. They consisted of three bars for heating and a plastic, artificial, coal-effect front. This was lit-up from behind in an attempt to give the impression that it was a real coal fire. Unfortunately, Gran never got round to removing the small brass companion set that was used to attend the real coal fire, which consisted of a little shovel, a hand brush, and a poker. These appliances all hung from a brass stand. Hurrying in from the cold one day, she grabbed the poker and started to poke the artificial coals, shattering the plastic front. They had only had it for a week. Poor Gran!

*****

My favourite 'Gran' story, by far, is this…

One Christmas, during the War, Grans' daughters, (my Aunties) Irene and Avis, were home on leave. Irene was in the Army and Avis was in the 'Wrens' (Navy). As it was too far for my Mother to travel home to Scotland, she joined them. I believe my Father was stationed in India at the time, so he was not present… Now, my crazy, Scottish

Grandmother, probably jealous because Mum had gone to Manchester instead of home, phoned the Inverness police and told them that Dad had kidnapped my Mother and put her to work in a brothel run from Grans' home in Manchester. She omitted to mention that they were married. The Inverness police contacted the Manchester police and asked them to look into it. This resulted in three large coppers bursting into Gran's, only to be confronted by three young women, lounging about in dressing gowns.

My Grandparents, Aunts and Mum were marched down to the local police station, but not before Gran had put on her fur coat; this was her pride and joy! She loved it! I have seen her attending weddings on hot summer days wearing it, along with a blue turban-like hat; the sweat streaming down her face.

The conversation in the police station went something like this:

Police Sergeant: Now, Mrs McClure, are you a madam?
Gran (thinking he meant are you a "lady") puffed herself up inside her fur coat and replied: I most certainly am! (She obviously thought it was posh voice time.)
Police Sergeant: Are these your girls?
Gran: They most certainly are.
Grandad (head in hands was heard to mutter): For God's sake, Avis. Shut the Hell up!

(My Aunty Avis was named after Gran.) After some confusion, Mum and my Aunts produced their Forces' Identity Papers and the matter was resolved.

Walking back home through the snow, Gran turned to Grandad and said, "William, what's a brothel?"

My Grandads' reply has gone unrecorded.

*****

My first memory is of crawling about on the lawn of a walled garden; I can distinctly remember seeing tall flowers bordering the wall; I now know these to be Lupins. This must have been Walnut Farm in Sale, Cheshire. However, it was known as 'Murky Manor' to the locals, for reasons to be explained later. My Father was a butcher by trade and had rented the old farm house whilst he plied his trade locally. It was at this point my sister, Jean, came along, eleven months my junior.

My Father could not understand why the rent for the old farm house was so cheap, though he was soon to find out. It would appear that the place harboured more ghosts than a Stephen King novel! None of which helped out with the rent. My Aunties, Uncles and Grandparents often told of the many sightings of various apparitions and of hearing unaccompanied footsteps… We had everything except the headless horseman. Hence the cheap rent! The locals would not go near the place.

It seemed that I had my own personal ghost in the form of an old hag; a black figure that was often seen kneeling beside my cot. My cot was moved to various rooms but the figure always followed. Indeed, when we left the farm for Yorkshire, she decided to come along for the ride. More on her later…

The next stop on my journey through life was to a mining village called Grimethorpe on the outskirts of Barnsley, South Yorkshire. I was to spend the next fourteen years of my life here.

Dad had secured a job with the Co-op as a butcher. The shop was on the High Street nestled between the Co-op, grocery and drapers' shops. It was a 'live in' position, and Dad managed the shop. I would be three or four years old at this time, then along came my second sister, Sheena.

Our living room and kitchen were attached to the back of the shop, with three bedrooms and a bathroom sitting above the shop. We also had an attic and a very scary cellar. At the back of the shop was a yard that housed an old, communal washhouse, complete with a massive stone sink (great for keeping newts in) and a metal stand where a brass coal boiler had once stood. There was also an old outside toilet.

Every room in that house had an open fireplace with the exception of the bathroom; it was our only form of heating. The problem was, unlike the local miners that received a monthly coal allowance, we didn't, and we struggled just to keep the living room fire going. Of course, if there was no fire, there was no hot water. God, it was a cold house!

I remember little of attending Infant School. Only that it consisted of a row of wooden huts situated behind the Junior School. These schools were literally right across the road from our shop, so, I didn't have far to go. In fact, if I looked out of my bedroom window, I would look right out onto the Junior School. It was an impressive brick building that bore high on its frontage, a large stone shield that proclaimed in large letters:

GRIMETHORPE JUNIOR SCHOOL 1903.

I can see it now.

I eventually entered through the school's mighty portals aged seven, and found very little to interest me. I only enjoyed English, Art and History. I hated Maths and still do. To this day, I am unable to do mental arithmetic; I cannot keep score for a darts match, and, therefore, I don't play darts. It is embarrassing! I can never remember telephone numbers either. Of the various cars I have owned, I can only remember the letters on the registration plates and not the numbers. I must have some form of dyslexia when it comes to numbers; either that, or I am just plain stupid. Hmm…hang on…I have just spelled 'dyslexia', so I can't be that stupid…!

The School graded its pupils A, B, C, and R. The highest being A, and R being the lowest. In fact, I believe R could have stood for 'Retarded'. Otherwise, why not just have A, B, C, and D? Are you still with me?

Anyway, I was classified as 'Retarded'. Upon being informed of this, my Mother nodded her head sagely and declared that she had always known.

"I tell everyone it is not your fault," she smiled kindly. "It's because your brain was starved of oxygen when you were born."
"What! You are going about telling everyone that I am fucking retarded!?"

I remember all the classrooms opened onto a central Hall where we assembled in the morning for prayers. I clearly remember the Lowry prints on the walls. We received a bottle of milk in the morning which contained a third of a pint. Rationing had only ended the year before (1954), and the Government was concerned about the growing number of kids getting rickets: a condition brought about by a lack of vitamins, hence the free milk. The only problem with the milk was that the 'milk break' was not until ten in the morning and the milkman left the milk in crates outside. So, in summer it would be curdled by the time we got it. However, we were still made to drink it. On really hot sunny days, the classrooms would be engulfed in a wave of vomit. No wonder they were always advertising for cleaners!

I made one particular friend whilst at Junior School: his name was Ian. He was the only child to a miner and his

Welsh wife. Being an only child, he was spoilt rotten; he got everything he wanted.

My Dad made me a cricket bat. He was very clever with his hands and could make anything, as you will later discover. I was playing cricket with Ian in his front garden - just myself and Ian. I went into his house to use the toilet and, on my return, I found Ian sat on the small wall that bordered his garden, minus the cricket bat. I asked him where it was and he replied that a big lad had snatched it from him and run off. He did not seem at all concerned and I knew that he was lying. If a big lad had gone anywhere near Ian, he would have gone crying to his mummy.

I pretended to accept his explanation and told him that I was going home. But what I actually did, was sneak round the corner and I watched him. Sure enough, he went into the house and came back out with MY bat! He perched on the wall with his back to me and, with an air of smugness, examined his prize. Silently, I crept up behind him and tapped him on the shoulder. The look of surprise when he turned was almost comical! I smacked my fist into his face and his nose exploded.

Grabbing my bat, I ran like hell. So…that was the end of that friendship…! A kid who had everything could not bear to see a kid who had nothing with a cricket bat that his Dad had made for him. (I was tempted to include the little shits surname whilst writing this…!)

Another thing I remember about my earlier years in Junior School, was when I was given a pair of boots with metal studs on the sole. These were supplied free to needy children by the Co-operative Society (my Dads' employer). I also believe that Boots Chemists ran a similar scheme. Rather apt, I thought. They were excellent for sliding on the ice and I was grateful for them.

Meanwhile at home, the babies kept arriving. Stewart was next, followed by Steve. It was like living in a bloody rabbit hutch!

On the subject of rabbits… I remember pedalling my little three-wheeled bike, up and down the High Street outside the shop one day, when the cry of a new born baby came from my Mothers' bedroom window; I would have been about six at the time. A passing miner looked up startled.

"My Mum's having a baby," I explained.
"Has it got big ears and buck teeth?" he asked. Of course, he was implying that my Mother had the same capacity for breeding as a rabbit. However, at that age, I took him literally. Curiosity getting the better of me, I clambered up the stairs in my bloody big boots and burst into my Mothers' bedroom.
"Has it got big ears and buck teeth?" I asked excitedly.
"Get out!" she screamed. As I was closing the door, I heard her explaining to the midwife, Nurse Jenkins, "His brain was starved of oxygen when he was born, you know?" Strange woman my Mother…

One thing I will always be grateful to my Father for, is that when I was being christened in Manchester, my Mother wanted to name me 'Valentine' (because I was born on Valentine's Day). At the eleventh hour, he persuaded her to name me after her brother, Gordon. Can you imagine serving in the Army or working down the pit with a name like Valentine. My life would have been Hell! Thanks, Dad!

As mentioned previously, Dad was very skilled at making things and, because money was tight, he would begin making Christmas toys secretly, in the attic, around late summer. Of course, I was 'Santa's little helper' and was sworn to secrecy. Without the aid of electric tools, he would make the most amazing things, equal to, and often better than anything bought in a shop. He once made a Rocking Horse; not one of those things you see with the head and legs just cut out of a sheet of plywood. His horses' head and legs were shaped with a rasp out of solid wood. Its tail and mane were made by unravelling that thick sort of hairy string (which was my job on the project).

Mind you, I did enjoy burning a hole in the horses' arse with a hot poker so that the tail could be attached. (Yes, I wonder as well!) Sometimes, he would buy a second-hand bike and completely strip it, then wire wool all the old paint off before re-painting it. All the rust on the wheel spokes would be removed. New tyres, bike seat and perhaps a bell. Hey presto, new bike! Incidentally, guess who did all of the rust removal, wire wool-ing and sanding? Correct! Though not all of the toys were homemade, some were purchased.

The family had grown even larger… Ian and Kevin had joined the throng; that's seven kids! The last, Alan, was to follow later. Ironically, he did have long ears and buck teeth!

One Christmas, we cut it really fine. Dad had crafted two forts for Stewart and Steven. The forts were identical, apart from one had the battlements painted black, and the other green. We worked all night and into the early hours of the morning; the last thing to do was paint the forts. I would have been about eight years old at this time.

Having completed the painting, Dad and I gingerly carried them downstairs, of course, the paint was still wet. This would have been around 5am on Christmas morning, before I collapsed onto the bed I shared with two brothers. I vaguely remember Dad saying to me, "Stand guard over the forts. Don't let your brothers get out of bed before the paint is dry!"

Yeah right...!

We got away with it, but only just! But as good as Dad was, he did have one spectacular failure. He made my sister, Sheena, a doll one Christmas. I am unsure of what Dad's idea of beauty was, but this was the thing of nightmares. It looked not unlike *Chucky* from the horror movie of the same name; I would not go anywhere near it.

It was horrific! Yet Dad looked upon it admiringly. I begged him to consider my sisters' mental health and burn it...preferably under a crucifix with a priest present. He eventually relented and bought my sister a doll from the shop. You don't know it, Sheena, but I have saved you a fortune in therapy fees!

And Dads' doll? Well, the last I heard, it was being used in satanic rites somewhere in rural Sussex.

As a kid, I loved my toy soldiers. The first ones were made of lead and beautifully painted. They were made by a company called William Britain and cost sixpence each. A week's pocket money for me. So, Christmas was a time to add to my Army, which consisted of cowboys and Indians, knights on horseback, American GI's, and British 'Tommies'. You name it. We would often have set battles in the attic. Two-inch nails were fired from a metal toy field gun and a thick rubber band was used to add more power to the spring mechanism. Using this method, a nail could be lobbed the length of the attic, causing mayhem in the enemy ranks.

The problem with lead soldiers was that they were cast and their heads would often get knocked off and then had to be stuck back on with the aid of a match stick. The same company later made good quality plastic soldiers which, of course, were far more durable, but lacked the charm of the lead ones.

I have always had an affinity with the American Indians, long before it became trendy. Watching the old black and white cowboy films, I always felt that the Indians were in the right and I wanted them to win. Of course, they never did. Continuing on this theme, one Christmas I received a great Indian outfit; the leggings and jacket had those long tassels and were accompanied by a plastic tomahawk, bow and arrows, and best of all, an Indian headdress with a stunning array of coloured feathers. I loved it!

The best thing about helping Dad in the attic was that he could not very well make my Christmas present with me there (Hee hee!), so I was usually bought something from a shop!

Anyway, having been told in advance that I was getting the Indian outfit, I happened to mention this to the lads at school. Come Christmas Day, my Mother shouted up to me that there was someone at the door asking for me. Looking out of my bedroom window, I saw a line of about fifteen kids all dressed in (you got it!) bloody cowboy outfits! It seemed like I was the only Indian in town.

The bastards chased me down streets, over wood and dale. An hour later, I staggered into the house causing Dad to do a double take: I was covered in dirt; most of the feathers in the headdress were broken, and I had left my tomahawk behind somewhere. (I think it was in Tommy Renton's forehead.) My only consolation was that I had managed to get two arrows off: both into Tony Burns - you couldn't miss the fat git!

Incidentally, I still have that affinity with American Indians. Indeed, later in life, I backpacked around the United States and worked in an Indian bar in Canada. I even had an Indian girlfriend. So, I can tell you that they take no offence whatsoever to being called 'Indians'. They think this 'First Nations Native American' stuff is bollocks. And…so do I!

Occasionally, all of the children in the house would organise, what we called, a 'Peg Battle'. This entailed an equal number of siblings on each side of a bedroom behind makeshift barricades, then we would throw clothes pegs at each other. The pegs were the old wooden ones (Dolly pegs). Sometimes, to even the numbers out, Dad would be recruited.

One winter's night, in the midst of a 'Peg Battle', a loud knocking was heard. Dad went downstairs to the backdoor and I followed. There stood two uniformed policemen: one was quite elderly, the other young. "Excuse me, sir," began the elderly one, then stopped mouth agape. Dad was wearing one of those 'Kiss Me Quick' cowboy hats with the yellow fringe that you used to buy at the seaside and I was stood behind him with a saucepan on my head. Both Policemen took a step back and almost held hands.

"Yes?" inquired Dad.
Recovering, the policeman said, "There has been a complaint about noise, sir. Is everything alright?"
"Oh! Sorry about that, officer," replied Dad, "We are just having a Peg Battle."

"Sir?" queried the officer.

"Yes?!" nodded Dad. "You know when a group of you go into a bedroom and throw pegs at each other?"

Both officers took another step back, and this time, they did hold hands. Turning as one, they fled into the night.

"We will try to keep it down!" Dad shouted after them.

Strange policemen…!

*****

On the corner of the High Street stood a little detached house, only a matter of yards from where we lived. In this house lived a really nice, old lady. I never knew her name but she must have been in her eighties. Her dress was Victorian looking and she could often be seen in the hedgerows, gathering herbs, berries and nettles, and putting them into a small burlap bag. She was tiny, and her small, walnut-brown face was always ready with a smile; I think she was of Gypsy stock. In her backyard, she had a rabbit hutch containing two, large, white rabbits. I was only about five at the time when some older boys had told me that the old lady was a witch, and when she caught children, she turned them into rabbits. I didn't believe this, but when my sister, Jean, and I, used to sneak into her backyard to look at the rabbits, it added a hint of danger.

One day, I was happily playing with my soldiers, when Jean toddled in wearing her blue dungarees. She would be aged four.

"Gordon, let's go and see the 'wabbits'," she lisped.

"Not now, Jean, I am playing soldiers," I replied. "I will go with you to see the 'wabbits', I mean 'rabbits' later."

Jean scowled at me and said, "Well, I am going now!" She then stomped out of the room. Ten minutes or so passed, and I decide to go looking for her. Cautiously, I sneaked into the old lady's yard.

No Jean!

Looking into the rabbit hutch, I almost screamed; there were not two rabbits, but THREE! The two, big, white ones, plus a new, ginger coloured one.

Now, Jean had ginger hair…!

"Stay there, Jean!" I whispered to the ginger rabbit, "I will go and get Dad!"

Running into the Co-op shop where Dad worked, I cried, "Dad, Dad! The witch has turned Jean into a 'wabbit', I mean rabbit!"

Dad, who had a line of customers, mostly women, turned to them and said, "His brain was starved of oxygen when he was born, you know?"

They all nodded in unison.

Exasperated, I ran into the house. "Mum, Jean's a 'wabbit'!"

Just then, Jean walked in. I ran towards her and threw my arms around her. Jean, puzzled by this demonstration of brotherly love, (we usually fought like cat and dog) looked

to Mum for an explanation. "It's alright Jean, his brain was starved of oxygen when he was a baby."
For fuck's sake…!

Apparently, what had happened was that the old lady had seen Jean with the rabbits and invited her into the house. So, whilst I was running around in a panic, my sister was scoffing cake and drinking lemonade just a few yards away. The old lady had acquired a ginger rabbit since our last visit.

This nice old lady would occasionally give us bottles of homemade Ginger Beer. To this day, I have never tasted anything as delicious as her Ginger Beer. As I recall it, it was very cloudy with a real bite to it, far superior than the shop bought crap.

Years later, upon hearing that one of us had a bad chest, she gave Mum a black coloured tea cup full of goose fat for rubbing on the chest of the ailing child. Now, there was a men's hair cream called 'Brylcreem' which was very popular at the time. My brother, Steve, in a bid to improve his looks, and believing that this stuff was 'Brylcreem', smothered the goose fat onto his hair. Well, the goose fat hardened and Steve's red hair shone like a thousand suns: you needed a pair of sunglasses just to look at him. He must have looked like a new star to a distant planet! The goose fat had hardened rock solid - you could have hit him over the head with a sledgehammer and he would not have felt a thing! As my parents discussed how to handle this new phenomenon, Steve strutted about thinking he looked like a film star.

As helpful as ever, I suggested that we stand him in the corner and use him as a standard lamp, thus, saving on electricity. This brought a scowl from Steve. I didn't want to upset him too much; if he had head butted me, he would have killed me!

It took Dad weeks to get the fat out of his hair. I think he started off with a hammer and chisel…!

*****

As you may have gathered, Dad was a little crazy, but I preferred the word 'eccentric', as did Dad.

Being a large family, you can imagine transport posed a problem. One day, he came home with an old Second World War field ambulance - I am not making this up! It had some conversions made to it: the racks in the back that had once held stretchers had been removed; two long benches down both sides installed; and, thankfully, the white circle with a red cross on it had been painted over in green.

My sister, Jean, (I think it was Jean...she was the smart one in the family. She was the only one to go to Grammar School. In our family, going to Grammar School was the equivalent of going to University.) expressed the opinion that it was a shame that the red cross had been removed. On being asked "why?" she said that if we ever wanted to go somewhere fast, the red cross may prompt the police into providing us with an escort.

She was joking, well, I think she was joking. It's hard to tell in my family.

Looking at Dad, I saw him stroking his chin and going "Hmm…" He was actually considering restoring the red cross! As if the local populace didn't think we were a bunch of loonies anyway…my family riding about in a Second World War field ambulance, complete with a red cross, would definitely have confirmed their suspicions.

'The Van' as we now referred to it, did open up many venues for us. One summer's day, my Uncle Stan and Aunty Irene, along with my two cousins, David and Lynn, paid us a visit from Langley, Manchester. They were accompanied by my Aunty Avis and Uncle Bert, also from Manchester. David and Lynn were about the same age as myself and Jean. Mountains of sandwiches were made, bottles of pop packed, and flasks of tea prepared, then off we went to Ryhill Reservoir. Now, Ryhill Reservoir was a great place for kids: sticklebacks and tadpoles could be caught in the reservoir, canal and ponds; newts and frogs abounded; there was a vast, wooded area to play in - it had everything!

I have always loved being on or near water. Sea, lake, river – it's all the same to me. I like the solitude that water brings and the wonder of what lies beneath the surface. You can't get me off a boat.

After an hour or two of play, we settled down in a sunny glade to eat our picnic. It was a beautiful summer's day; the air hummed with the sound of insects and birdsong. Looking up, I noticed my cousin, Lynn, was eating a bread roll. Lynn was a skinny waif of a girl with long, blonde hair, and a mischievous way about her. I would have much rather had a bread roll than an ordinary bread sandwich. So, I began searching for one amongst the food laid out on the blanket. Lynn's seemed to have been the only roll...then I noticed a headless toadstool stalk next to her. It took some time for my brain to process this information. Then, pointing at Lynn, I squeaked, "Lynn, Lynn!" Fourteen pairs of eyes swung in her direction, then their brains went through the same processing as mine had gone through. Meanwhile, Lynn was happily chomping away on this large, brown toadstool! Before anyone could gather their wits, Lynn had finished eating her toadstool, smacked her lips, dusted her hands, and then reached for another one. Weird kid, Lynn...

There was some speculation amongst the adults that Lynn may have poisoned herself and she should be taken to Wakefield Hospital, but they settled on a 'let's wait and see' approach. So, Lynn, who was about eight at the time, was placed with her back against a tree, and we all stared at her in silence, waiting for something to happen. Lynn just stared right back at us. After about ten minutes, Uncle Stan, her father, went over and prodded her as if she was a dead mouse, then said, "She seems to be alright!" Indeed, she was. In fact, she looked so well, I was thinking of trying a toadstool myself!

I think it was at this time that I realised it wasn't just my branch of the family that were nuts. They were all nuts and I took great solace in this. We were not alone!

*****

It was around this time that I went into the bathroom and saw one of my red-haired brothers (either Ian or Steven) with a frog in the sink. He was filling the sink with hot water, he was not trying to harm the frog. He was trying to be kind to it; he thought that the frog would be happier in hot water rather than cold. Of course, with a frog being a cold-blooded creature, this had an adverse effect. It spread-eagled itself up the side of the sink in an attempt to escape the hot water. Then, like something out of a horror movie, it let out a very loud hissing sound; it scared the life out of me! My brother bolted and I very nearly followed him. Instead, I gradually lowered the temperature of the water so that the frog would not go into shock. It still amazes me that I had the presence of mind to do this, particularly as I was so young. I left it for some time in cold water, gently picked it up, and took it to a little duck pond behind the school. To my dismay, on release, it swam off dragging one leg behind it: it was obviously paralysed in one leg - funny the things you remember!

*****

I know this sounds strange, but another place Dad sometimes took us to play was a rubbish dump (I know!). It was only a ten minute drive away. So, occasionally, on a summer's evening after work, he would take us there in 'The Van'. It was on common land on the way to Great Houghton. The journey took us through a place called Brierley, and on a small Green there, we would often see Gypsies; I mean proper Romany ones in their old, round-roofed, horse drawn caravans, cooking on open fires with their ponies grazing close by. We always waved and they would wave back. Where have all these people gone?

The rubbish dump was not as bad as you might think; really it was an old quarry, surrounded by common land. A farm house with a duck pond could be seen in the near distance. It was amazing the stuff you could salvage there. Pram wheels for making buggies (or 'trolleys' as we used to call them). There was a particular pram that traded under the name of 'Silver Cross'. This had large wheels at the back, small wheels at the front and was ideal for making trolleys. I quickly mastered the art of trolley making.

I would often take my catapult to the dump for target practice. Stones would be launched at scurrying rats. They didn't fear me too much, although I did get a few.

One evening, on returning from the dump, we realised that my brother, Stewart, was missing. He would have been about seven years old at the time. I got the usual, "He is your brother and you should look after him. You are the eldest." Anyway, Dad and I set off back to the dump to find him. An hour had passed by this time, and, approaching the dump, we saw Stewart standing by the side of the road, crying. He was talking to a young couple who had pulled over on their motorbike and sidecar.

"Are you his father?" queried the young man quite angrily. "Yes," replied Dad, and was about to thank the couple for stopping when the young woman chipped in.
"He told us that you brought him to the rubbish dump and left him. You should be ashamed of yourself!"
"Oh! Come on, love," quipped Dad. "I have eight of them. You can't expect me to feed them all!"

What I would have given for a camera!

*****

Dad, in a moment of weakness, entrusted me with delivering the meat to his customers on a Saturday morning. The Co-op provided this really heavy bike with a basket on the front for holding the meat parcels. The round usually took about four hours.

One day, pedalling the heavy bike up Cemetery Hill, I noticed a coal lorry in front of me, and, trailing from the back of the lorry, was a rope. Trying to be clever, I grabbed the rope and looped it around the handlebars, the idea being that the lorry would tow me up the hill. On reaching the top of the hill, the lorry started to pick up speed, so I released the rope allowing it to pull clear of the handlebars. Unfortunately for me, there was a knot in the rope and as it was pulling clear, the knot caught between the handlebars and the brake lever. Unable to free the knot because of the tension, I had no choice but to hang on for dear life as the lorry sped on to its next stop. No amount of pedalling would give me enough slack to free the rope.

I was screaming, "Mister! Mister!" This caught the attention of passing pedestrians, and, on seeing my predicament, they burst into laughter. Indeed, one old lady with a stick had to sit on a wall she was laughing so much. I felt like a right dick! Eventually, the lorry stopped and I was able to free myself.

*****

A disturbing incident occurred whilst doing my meat round. There was one elderly lady that I delivered to who was partially blind. I will call her Mrs Fran. (Not her real name.) Due to her blindness, I was very careful to count her change into her hand, naming each coin as I did so.

One morning, she demanded that I cleared the ashes from her grate and remake her fire. She was quite abrupt, but I did not mind helping her out. This became a regular Saturday morning chore - I never received any thanks for this and she even resented me asking to use the sink to wash my hands. One Saturday afternoon, Dad called me into the shop and asked me if I knew anything about money going missing from Mrs Fran's home. He didn't state how much and I simply replied, "No." He just said, "OK." It appeared that Mrs Fran had entered our shop, and in front of other customers, had openly accused me of stealing £200. Now, £200 was a lot of money in the early sixties, especially when you consider that a face-worker down the pit was on £20 a week. A few days later, she entered the shop once more, and in a far quieter tone told Dad that she had found the money: no apology was offered.

The following Saturday I delivered her meat as usual. After counting out her change, I turned to leave. "Hey, you!" she said, "What about my fire?" I stared at her in disbelief. "I don't think so, Mrs Fran," I said, and left. Again, I was summoned to the shop. "Were you rude to Mrs Fran this morning?" asked Dad. "Not at all," I replied and went on to explain what had transpired. It was some time later that I found out what had happened. All I knew was that I was no longer to deliver to Mrs Fran's home. I was told by Dads' apprentice, Eric, that Mrs Fran had stormed into the shop and asked Dad if he had, "Put me right about making up her fire?" Dad told her, in no uncertain terms, that her custom was no longer welcome and that she was not to enter the shop again, as her behaviour was unacceptable.

I was very grateful to Dad for believing and trusting in me.

*****

My career as a meat delivery boy came to an abrupt end one terrible winter's morning. The snow was so deep I had to push the bike in many places. My round was taking a lot longer than it would normally; then I got a puncture so I couldn't ride at all. The next calamity occurred when I dragged the bike up onto its stand outside a house I was delivering to. The snow was drifting down, I was cold and hungry. Knocking on the door, I looked round and saw a large Alsatian up on its hind legs, sniffing at the basket. Then, suddenly, the bike went over and the dog ran off with a parcel of meat in its mouth! The remaining meat was scattered all over the pavement.

Righting the bike, I bent over to retrieve the meat. On doing so, all the loose change in the leather satchel I carried, fell out into the deep snow; I had neglected to secure the catch. I had to carefully put my fingers down each hole in the snow to retrieve the coins. I somehow managed to complete the round. I was pissed off! Back at the shop, Dad said, "Where the Hell have you been? You should have been back hours ago?" That was the final straw. "You can keep your stupid job!" I declared, steaming off. Dad's jaw dropped open in amazement. I didn't care, I had two paper rounds anyway.

*****

In Grimethorpe, there was an old picture house called 'The Palace'. It was anything but! However, it served its purpose. This was managed by a man named Jerve. I don't know if that was his surname or Christian name. Jerve was immense in size. This was a time when you rarely saw fat people. He always wore a rather tatty, three-piece suit and a flat cap. Jerve seemed to do everything at this cinema: he sold the ice cream; he sold the tickets, and I believe that he was also the projectionist: he was a one man show. He was also a very nice man. I recall having a barking cough one day and he kindly took me to one side and wrote down a cure for my condition on a piece of paper to give to Mum. I only remember that it involved vinegar. He then produced a half-eaten packet of mints from his pocket and gave them to me. I never forgot the kindness he showed me that day.

One of the perks of Dad having the shop, though it wasn't actually his, was that the picture house provided him with a free pass in exchange for displaying a poster featuring that week's films. Of course, being one of eight kids, you had to wait seven weeks for your turn.

The picture house hosted a Saturday afternoon matinee where it cost sixpence to get in. This posed a problem for me as I only got twopence a day, plus sixpence on Saturday as pocket money (old money). This was long before I had my meat and paper rounds. My mates were lucky as they had local grandparents, aunties and uncles to scrounge money off, but all mine lived in far-off Scotland and Manchester. If I didn't want to give up my Saturday sixpence, the only other way I could secure my admittance fee was by scrounging round for empty pop bottles. These could be taken back to the shop where the twopence deposit fee would be returned. See, that's how you recycle. Easy innit?

My only other option was to sell one of the pet mice that I bred. Conveniently, these sold for sixpence.

One way or another, I usually made it to the matinee. They would usually show a number of cartoons, usually Micky Mouse, or such like, followed by a Western. Frequently starring Gene Autry, Roy Rogers, The Cisco Kid, and my favourite, Johnny Mack Brown. (Who?) The matinee always ended with a serial, commonly Zorro or Flash Gordon. The hero was typically left hanging off a cliff (literally a cliff-hanger ending) to entice you back next week to see if they had survived, which they always somehow managed.

On your admission ticket was a long number. In the intermission, Jerve would get up onto the stage and draw from a bag containing all the ticket stubs. If your number came up, you claimed the prize. Much to my delight one Saturday, I'd won! It was a really big bar of chocolate. I think it was the first time I had ever won anything. Mum, at the time, was bedridden with a new baby. I can't remember which one - it was difficult to keep count!

I thought I would give Mum the chocolate, she would thank me and say how clever I was. I was only a little kid. Excited, I made my way home, followed by a gaggle of kids trying to scrounge chocolate off me. I ran the gauntlet and arrived home, chocolate bar intact. For some reason, Mums' bed was in the living room. Hardly able to contain myself, I ran into the living room and said, "Mum, Mum, look what I have won for you!" She glared at me and said, "Don't you ever come barging in here like that again. Put the chocolate on the side and get out!" Remember, this what not her bedroom, it was the living room. Well, this was too much for me; anger and resentment welled up inside. Throwing the chocolate down, I said something like, "You could have said 'thank you'. I hate you!"

The next thing I knew, a Wellington boot was spinning through the air, almost in slow motion. I turned to my right to escape and it struck my left ear with a tremendous thud. I was wearing the boots with studs that I mentioned earlier. These shot out from under me and I went crashing down. It was a bit of a blur after that, but I was in great pain with my ear for days. So much so, that my Mother had to take me to the Doctor. His name was Doctor Foster, (no really!) who was a very large Scotsman. He held a surgery in a house on the High Street.

He examined my ear and asked me when the trouble started. I answered truthfully that it started when Mum threw a Wellington boot at me and it hit me on the ear. Mum gave me a quick kick on the ankle and suddenly exaggerated her Scottish accent, hoping to curry favour with the Doctor. "What can you do with kids, hey Doctor? Always making things up. He took a fall, Doctor."

This was partially true, I did take a fall, but only after being hit by the boot. I could tell that the good Doctor saw straight through her. All the way home she berated me. "Fancy telling the Doctor something like that!" For the rest of my life, I have had trouble with my left ear and I was very fortunate to be accepted into the Army.

*****

I cannot write about my childhood without mentioning 'Woolley Edge'. We called it 'Woolley Edge' because it was a small, wooded area with rocky outcrops, situated on the edge of a small mining village called Woolley. I loved going there and found it a magical place where my imagination could take flight. Many an imagined dragon has been killed there with a stick for a sword. It inspired me to write my first poem: *The Battle of Woolley Edge* (which I have included in this book).

In the early sixties, the Co-op did a full renovation on the shop, and turned the house into a flat. The flat spread across the top of all three shops: the grocers; butchers, and drapers. We still only had three bedrooms, but we managed to save the attic, though it now had to be accessed by means of a trapdoor. So, we had to acquire a ladder.

We now had only two open fires: one in the living room and one in my parents' bedroom. I never saw the one in the bedroom lit. Still, no central heating. That flat never did get any central heating.

The bedrooms were allocated as such:

My parents had their own room, of course.

My two sisters had a room with a double bed.

Myself, and five brothers, shared a room with two double beds in it, so, three to a bed. Unless someone wet the bed, then it was six to a bed. We had one pillow between us. No pillowcase - just the pillow - an old thing that was so flat it was like putting your head on a towel, yet we still fought over it. Eventually, we agreed to take it in turns. The strange thing was, you might have gone to sleep with it, but you never woke up with it. That damn pillow must have done the rounds between the two beds at least once during the course of a night.

Nowadays I can't sleep unless I have three, good quality pillows under my head. I sleep almost upright.

Keeping the flat warm was a constant battle. We would burn anything: old shoes, bones from the shop, anything. Dad and I would, in winter, resort to going down to the pit waste heaps, to salvage what we could. Now, this was illegal. Although these mountains of waste from the mines might have been rubbish, it was rubbish belonging to the Coal Board. We would take the shop bike with the cradle on the front that usually held the basket, two sacks, and set off; always at night, of course, to avoid detection. To get to the waste heap, you had to navigate your way down Pit Lane. It was a fair way - maybe a quarter of a mile. Pit Lane was simply a cinder track that started at the pit baths and wound its way down to the waste heaps. Unfortunately for us, the track ended in a steep downward slope making our return journey, laden with pickings, a lot harder.

Dad pedalled with me perched on the cradle, tyres crunching on the cinder, as we made our way through the darkness. On arrival, we would search through the slag and shale looking for small lumps of coal, hidden in the cast-off detritus, like a couple of gold prospectors searching for the mother lode.

Once we found a 'vein', I would hold the sacks open whilst Dad filled them by hand. Once the two sacks had been filled, we secured the necks with string. This took some time as we worked without torches. Then we would heft a sack onto the bikes cradle. Dad would push the bike up the steep slope, mounting it at the top before cycling home. I would be left behind with the remaining sack, waiting for him to return. This would take at least half an hour.

The night air would be full of strange sounds and I would hide in a large, concrete pipe, clutching my little penknife for protection. It had a half-inch blade, so what protection it would have actually given me, I don't know. I was particularly afraid of the rats: I never saw them, but I could hear them.

I would look up at the stars, dreaming of foreign lands and adventure. Just how I would get there was a mystery. Little did I know, that in the not-too-distant future, I would find a solution.

On the subject of stars, it was on one of these nights that Dad pointed out The Plough to me, sometimes known as The Big Dipper. Once the seven stars in The Plough are located, it is easy to find the North Star. Dad explained that wherever you are in the world, if you follow the North Star you will eventually reach home.

Whatever country I have been in, I have always looked for the North Star.

Eventually Dad would return. I could hear the crunch of tyres getting nearer and nearer in the still of the night. Together, we would push the final load up the slope, then, with me perched on the sack, we'd pedal our way home.

*****

Nearing my eleventh birthday, my life was to change considerably for the better. I was kicking an old, leather football against the air raid shelter at the bottom of a piece of waste ground that was once a park. Looking up, I saw Dad, hunched up in his overcoat, hurrying by. It was a cold evening in February.

"Hey, Dad!" I shouted. No response. He must not have heard me.

"Hey, Dad!" I shouted again. He half turned, and out from beneath his coat, the little, black head of a puppy poked out. I had begged Dad for a puppy for my birthday and there it was. He had been trying to conceal it from me until my birthday in a few days' time.

Rex was a medium-sized dog with a lot of terrier in him. He sported a black head, and a white body with two large black spots on his rump. I adored him and he was all mine. He was absolutely fearless. He never caused fights with other dogs, but he would fight any dog regardless of its size that went for him. I never saw him run away from a fight.

He had two enemies in particular and both of these were border collies. I would hold him on a leash to try and keep him away from these dogs, but that didn't stop them from attacking. In fact, my holding him back only impeded him. So, I would set him loose and leave him to it, knowing that he would eventually catch up with me.

Rex was a funny eater. I would put food down and he would just sniff at it and walk away. In most families at that time, dogs ate the leftovers from the family table. They were not spoilt like they are nowadays. I used to buy him canned dog food out of my paper round money and boil up scraps from the shop for him. But he just didn't seem interested in food.

The other thing was that I can never remember him barking; he would growl, but not bark. We were inseparable, we really were. Apart from school, he never left my side. Some of my siblings tried to win him over, but he remained loyal to me. Dad wanted him to sleep in the living room, but he would scratch at the door until being allowed to sleep on an old coat beside my bed.

This is how brave he was. I was playing cricket in a park and Rex was with me. A fat, bowlegged man with an equally fat, bowlegged bull mastiff, walked into the park. The mastiff launched a completely unprovoked attack on Rex. After a short, fierce fight, the mastiff had its jaws locked around Rex's throat. Rex lay still but the mastiff still held on. I could see blood stains forming around his neck and thought that he was dead. I was crying and trying to prise the mastiff's jaws open with the handle of my cricket bat. I begged the man to get his dog off. He just stood there and never said a word. I thought, 'Fuck this!' and still, believing Rex was dead, I lifted my cricket bat and was about to brain the mastiff when the fat man pushed me aside and got his dog off.

Both man and dog bowlegged it up the park. I held Rexs' head in my arms and sobbed my heart out. Then, to my surprise, he opened his eyes, jumped up and set off after the man and his dog at full pelt. They were about a hundred yards away at this time and the last thing they expected was this black and white thunderbolt hurling towards them. They were oblivious to Rex's approach until he took a chunk out the mastiffs' rump. The dog yelped and jumped up in the air, causing the man to follow suit. Rex then turned and bolted back towards me. This spectacle had all the kids in the park folding over with laughter. The man and his dog, having strutted up the park, proud of what they had done, were now a laughing stock. Their dignity, if they ever had any in the first place, was now in tatters. I opened my arms for Rex to run into, but he ran straight past me, and he didn't stop until he had reached home. You had to love him!

*****

Rex and Mum had a really strange relationship - they completely ignored each other. I am surprised that they didn't walk into each other; they just didn't see each other. As I have mentioned, Rex wasn't a barker, but if Mum made a physical move to hit me, he would emit a very low rumbling sound. It wasn't exactly a growl, but it was a warning that she heeded. I would not say she was afraid of him, but they seemed to have an understanding: the message was clear.

Our backyard led down to two, big, wooden gates, giving access to the back of the shops. Rex's favourite position was to sit outside these gates in the passage way that ran behind the buildings. On this occasion, the gates were closed so that he had to sit behind the gates looking through the slats.

I was looking out of the kitchen window and I noticed a young lad approach him. This lad dropped to his knees and spat into Rex's face through the slats. A startled Rex responded by shoving his muzzle between the slats and biting him on the nose. The lad ran off and told his parents that Rex had bitten him in an unprovoked attack. This resulted in his angry parents confronting Dad and there was talk of police action. This could have resulted in Rex being put down.

I told his parents what I had witnessed, pointing out that it would not have been possible for such a small dog to have bitten him on the nose had their son not have been kneeling down. Later, the police made a visit to speak with Dad, which put me in fear for Rex's life. So, I devised a plan. The plan was for me to run away with Rex to provoke some public sympathy and, hopefully, some Press coverage. Thus, saving him from the gallows. Cunning, yes?

The following Saturday, I gathered an old blanket, a billy can I had made for brewing tea leaves in, (no tea bags then), and a box of matches. A search of the larder came up blank, but not to worry, I didn't expect to be away too long anyway.

My plan was for a search party to eventually find us and, in that way, gain some publicity. I made a point of telling two of my brothers that I was going up into the woods with Rex and that I would be back at about 6pm. I even told them what part of the woods I was going to. They wanted to come with me, but, of course, I had to refuse them.

On the outskirts of Grimethorpe is a wood that we called 'Lady Wood' and this was to be our destination. I knew every tree in that wood. Rex and I went there at every opportunity: running through the trees, making shelters and baking potatoes pinched from the fields on camp fires. I was a regular Ray Mears.

Finding a nice spot, I erected a shelter made of branches and ferns, and quickly had a fire going. I could get a fire going even in the wettest of conditions.

We had left the flat at about ten that morning and I wasn't expecting anyone to come looking for us until dark when my parents would begin to wonder where we were. So, having some time to kill, we went in search of rabbits. Soon it was dark, I built up the fire and we sat in the shelter with the blanket around us, waiting for rescue. "Not be long now, Rex!" I said, starting to feel hungry. I could see the headlines in the Barnsley Chronicle:

'LOCAL BOY RUNS AWAY WITH DOG TO SAVE ITS LIFE!'

Brilliant!

Around midnight, I was expecting to see torches flashing and hear people shouting my name. I built the fire up so that it could be seen. Surely my brothers had told them where I had gone? My parents must be sick with worry? Well, Dad anyway…? I had borrowed two shillings off him the day before…

My stomach was starting to rumble, so was Rexs', and I didn't like the way he was looking at me. Just to be on the safe side, I thought I had better stay awake. I got out my penknife just to remind him that I had it. He was still looking at me strangely and licking his lips. I was beginning to feel nervous. "I am doing this for you!" I reminded him, "Where the Hell are they?"

Dawn found us huddled up together under the blanket; we must have fallen asleep. I was relieved to find myself on this side of Rex's stomach. "Oh! I get it!" I explained to a very pissed off looking dog, "They are waiting for daylight to complete a thorough search." On saying this, I built the fire up and threw on damp, green ferns to create smoke. I had done everything but send them a bleeding telegram!

Surely they would be here soon and they would hail me as a hero. I would give them until midday…

Now, I was really hungry and was beginning to imagine a skinned and gutted Rex roasting slowly on a spit over the camp fire.

Midday came and went, so, head bowed, I trudged home with Rex in my wake. I was expecting the biggest bollocking of my life.

Nothing. Zilch.

I was eleven years old and had been absent all night. I had been away for twenty six hours and none of the bastards had even missed me! I believe Jean had mentioned around midnight that she had not seen Rex for a while. Charming! Then, to add insult to injury, Dad asked if I had the two shillings that I owed him!

The good news was that the lads' parents had decided that they would not pursue the matter. So, Rex lived to bite another day. What a boy will do for his dog!

*****

One dreadful day, Rex was hit by a car. We were heading for the woods and I was trying to put him on the leash. He was running around excitedly and ran out onto the road. A car hit him with a tremendous thump and spun him into the air. The cars wing had struck him on the shoulder and I feared the worst. To my relief, he got up quickly, ran towards me whimpering, and I thought for a moment that he was alright. On reaching me, he collapsed at my feet.

The car never stopped but it wasn't their fault. It slowed right down after the collision, and on seeing Rex run off, the driver must have thought that he was OK and sped off.

I carried Rex into the flat and laid him out on a table, sending one of my brothers down to the shop for Dad. I was in a real state, sobbing my heart out. Dad brought calm and set about examining him. It appeared his left shoulder and leg were very badly bruised, though it was his paw that caused the most concern. I begged Dad to take him to the Vets but he just didn't have the money. It took weeks of nursing before he was anything like his former self. His paw never did mend properly, and for the rest of his life, every third or fourth step resulted in a limp.

*****

One of my most endearing memories of Rex was when I returned home on leave from the Army. I had enlisted in 1965, and after a three month training period in Shrewsbury, Shropshire, I was sent to join my Regiment in the troubled Port of Aden (then Saudi Arabia).

On my return, I was given a Railway Warrant to Barnsley and three weeks leave. I had not seen my family or Rex for eight months. Now in those days, to travel on a warrant you had to wear full dress uniform. Getting off the bus in Grimethorpe, I headed for the flat, lugging my heavy,

Army suitcase, full of presents for the family. Approaching the back passageway that led down to the flat, I was delighted to see Rex sitting in his usual place outside the gate. From the top of the passageway, I shouted, "Rex!" His head turned to look at me, then turned away. Again, I shouted, "Rex!" His head spun towards me, and giving a yelp, he bolted up the passage. Nearing me, he launched himself, landing on my chest, and into my arms. My hat went skittering and he almost knocked me over. He was wriggling about, whimpering, crying and licking my face. It took me ten minutes to calm him down. He had not recognised me in my uniform.

I entered the flat with Rex glued to my heels. Seeing Mum in the kitchen washing dishes, I said, "Hello, Mum." She turned towards me and replied "Oh! Hello." No hug. No 'would you like a cup of tea?' Nothing…

Discovering that my brothers were in the woods camping, I quickly changed into my tracksuit, and after saying hello to Dad in the shop from whom I received a better welcome, Rex and I set off for the woods. I was very fit and even Rex had trouble keeping up with me as we raced through the trees in search of my brothers.

We were together again; a boy and his dog.

I was living in Bristol, and one, fateful, November night, I phoned Dad from a public phone box. He told me that Rex was dead. I should not have been surprised; he was an old dog - possibly fourteen years old - but I was. I thought he was indestructible. The hurt was so great that I was unable to cry. I should have been there with him at the end.

After all these years, he still visits me in my dreams. Then together, once again, we would run wild through the woods.

*****

My story cannot be told without more than a mention of my Aunty Avis and Uncle Bert. They lived in Moss Side, Manchester. They had no children and lived happily in an end of terrace house along with their dog, Kim. I believe Bert was a Londoner and had met Avis (my Dad's sister) during the War. They would often visit us in Grimethorpe, and sometimes, we would visit them in Manchester.

Being so many of us, sleeping arrangements were a nightmare. I would wake up in the morning and look about me, the living room would be strewn with sleeping bodies; it looked like the aftermath of the Battle of the Little Big Horn.

They always bought us Christmas presents; it must have cost them a fortune. One Christmas, I received from them a present no child really wants: a book. But this book opened up a whole new world to me. It was *A Christmas Carol* by Charles Dickens. After my initial disappointment, I settled down to read it and I didn't stop until I had finished it. That book kindled my passion for reading and now I must always have a book at hand.

I have spoken to people that have boasted that they have never read a book in their lives. They are actually proud of the fact. You sad bastards!

Fortunately for me, the Junior School across the road had converted a small room into a public library. It was only open two nights a week and housed only a few hundred books. It was staffed by a man in his thirties, always smartly dressed in a suit. He would come to see a lot of me over the years.

I would have been about ten years old when I joined the library. My taste in reading included: H. Rider Haggard; Dickens; Robert Louis Stevenson; H. G. Wells; Conan Doyle, and Mark Twain.

A few years later, I would read John Steinbeck's: *Of Mice and Men*, and went on to read everything he ever wrote. Even at that age I recognised a master craftsman when I saw one.

Years later, I found myself visiting my American girlfriend in San Francisco, California. She had a sister living in Salinas and she asked me to join her on a visit. Salinas is the birthplace of Steinbeck, and many of his books were written there. As I walked the streets of Salinas, I thought of Steinbeck's fictional characters in Cannery Row: Doc, Mac and the boys, who had their escapades on the shores of the Pacific Ocean, just seven miles away.

Another author I admire is Laurie Lee. He is known, of course, for his autobiography *Cider with Rosie*, but this British author has written many books and poems. A completely different style of writing to Steinbeck, but both authors knew how to develop their characters and make you care about them. I love the poetic, lyrical way in which Lee writes. I don't think he ever got the recognition he deserves. How do these writers do it? It makes me ashamed to pick up a pen.

Sorry, I digress. Back to Avis and Bert.

*****

As we got older, some of us would make personal coach trips to Manchester to visit them. This would include a day out with our Grandparents. These trips must have been inconvenient at times but we were always made welcome.

It was on one such visit in March 1963 that I heard The Beatles' *Please Please Me* for the first time. I was fifteen and working at the pit. I went into a coffee bar on Main Road, near the then Manchester City ground. I ordered a coffee and a pastry, then studied the contents of the juke box. I selected The Beatles' *Please Please Me*. I had not heard it before as it had just come out. This terrific sound washed over me and the hairs on my arms stood up. It was a shilling for three selections, or a 'bob' as we called it.

I played the record another three times, then I played it yet another three times. The cafe owner was going nuts. "Don't play that record again," he growled. We had an argument. My point was that it was my money and I should be able to choose what I wanted to play. He told me to "Piss off out!" He was a big bugger and I didn't fancy my chances, so I put another 'bob' in and quickly selected *Please Please Me* another three times before fleeing. How embarrassing being thrown out of a coffee bar! A pub, yes, but a coffee bar! I have been a great lover of The Beatles ever since.

*****

Another nice gesture that Avis and Bert performed was on our eleventh birthdays, when we children would all receive a watch from them. Mine was a square faced Timex. This was my first ever watch and I treasured it for years.

*****

Back with the McClure family, Bonfire Night was a time I always looked forward to. It was the weeks of preparation that went into it: dragging the trolley up into the woods for dead logs and going around the houses collecting junk to burn. Remember there were no so-called recycling centres in those days, so households would welcome your autumn visit. It would give them the opportunity for a good clear out of old mattresses, wardrobes, armchairs, couches…you name it. This practise also stopped fly-tipping. OK, so these fires caused smog, there was always smog the day after Bonfire Night, but what do you think happens to all these items when carted off to a recycling centre? My guess is that they are burnt…

For scrap iron there was always the rag and bone man with his horse and cart. If you were lucky, he would give you a balloon. Recycling sixties style. Easy innit?

Pocket money was saved for fireworks and Dad provided a small box. Chestnuts were collected from the woods. I would spend hours making a 'Guy Fawkes'. My 'Guys' were not just a bunch of rags, they were a work of art; it often pained me to burn them. There were times when my siblings had to wrestle them from me and drag them to the fire. Barbarians!

Once the Bonfire had burnt down to cinders, we would throw potatoes into the ashes to bake, and roast chestnuts on a shovel. I think I probably preferred Bonfire Night to Christmas.

*****

I promised earlier that I would return to what I called the 'Old Hag'. Some sort of spirit that I believe followed the family, particularly me, from 'Murky Manor' to Grimethorpe. This apparition, not only followed me to Grimethorpe, but around the world. This went on for years until I was finally able to rid myself of her. By no means were these nightly visits, they were very spontaneous - perhaps ten times a year. Thinking back if there was a trigger for these visits, they did seem to occur when I was feeling particularly down or low. Her visits were always heralded by a strange noise: a kind of white, static noise that started low, then rose to a crescendo in waves. I could never understand why, if there was someone else in bed with me, they were never woken by it.

Once the noise abated, the 'Old Hag' would appear kneeling beside my bed. She was very small, dressed in a black shift or gown, with a black hood that obscured most of her face. In fact, though I have always referred to this spectre as 'she', it could have been a 'he', as I could only make out the nose and eyes in the shadows of the cowl. But something told me it was female and malevolent. I would lay paralysed in bed and all I could do was wait until she left, which she would after about a minute. She never spoke or moved; she just looked at me. Over the years, I grew less and less afraid of her. When I was about twenty three years old, I just told her to "Fuck off!" and, to my amazement, she did! Very occasionally over the years, she would risk a visit, but I would just tell her to "Fuck off!" again, and she would!

On writing, it's been about thirty years since she's honoured me with a visit. I kind of miss the old bitch. Reflecting on this phenomenon, I often wondered if she fed on my fear. So, when I no longer feared her, she had nothing to feed on. You can analyse these things forever, but at the end of the day, it is just better to let sleeping dogs lie.

*****

The year 1967 saw me in Berlin with my Battalion. It was a volatile period because of the Cold War with Soviet Russia.

This was a two year posting and I had recently married. I was dismayed to hear that I was not eligible for married quarters and that no home leave would be granted during this posting. I found this unacceptable and devised a plan to bring my wife over. Learning some basic German from a friends' wife who was German, I set off to find private accommodation. We were barracked in a place called Kladow, on the outskirts of the city. It was more like a village than a suburb with lakes and woods. This is where I secured a bedsit and flew my wife over at my own expense. The Army was not pleased with me taking the initiative (I assume for security reasons) but there was little they could do about it. My wife was a civilian.

After a year in the bedsit, just after my twentieth birthday, the Army provided us with temporary married quarters. These quarters were once Second World War German barracks that the Army had converted. There would be about six servicemen and their families living there, including us. This accommodation consisted of two rooms: one was a living room with a sink and a cooker in the corner; the other room, the bedroom, was situated next door. So, to go to bed, you had to exit the living room and walk down the corridor to the next door down, which would be the bedroom.

You can imagine the scene late at night, when everyone was walking up and down the corridor going to their respective bedrooms. Shouts of "Night, Jack! Night, Sue!

Night, Jim! Night, Ann!" It was like living with the bloody Walton's!

Under these rooms was a cellar that ran the full length of the building. It was accessed by going down a long flight of stone steps. The cellar was vaulted and had a series of archways running down the middle forming open sections. The walls were covered in graffiti left by German soldiers, along with some quite impressive artwork. The only lighting was emergency lighting; just a few caged bulbs scattered about the ceiling giving off very little light. I am guessing at one time this place was used for storing ammunition, but by this time, it housed the circuit and fuse boxes for the whole building.

It was not uncommon at peak times, when everyone had their electrical appliances going, for the electricity to trip. This would result in myself, or one of the other lads shouting, "I'll get it!" and going down to the cellar to reset the trip switch.

One night I volunteered and made my way to the fuse box, with only the emergency lighting to guide me. I reset the switch and suddenly, I felt a presence behind me. Turning, I saw the form of a German soldier. He could only have been fourteen years old at the most. He wore a forage cap and a grey greatcoat that was far too big for him; the sleeves covering his hands.

After my initial start, and realising he was a ghost, I asked him in German, "Are you alright? Can I help you?" I received no reply. He just stared; not necessarily at me, but in my direction. His grey eyes held a terrible sadness about them and I repeated my questions, again, receiving no response.

I made to leave which meant passing within a few feet of him. Just as I was passing, I said, "Gute nacht" (Goodnight). As I did so, I saw that he was beginning to fade. These things do not usually bother me, but this one did. I carried an air of sadness about me for days; I just couldn't shake it off. I never told anyone of my sighting. After this experience, I returned to the cellar many times to reset the trip switch, but I never saw this young soldier again. I hope he found peace.

*****

A terrible time in my life was 1998. My wife and I had separated after sixteen years together; the situation wasn't helped when the company I worked for closed down and I was made redundant.

After spending twenty, for the most part happy, years in Chichester, West Sussex, I left and wandered about the States and Canada, like the lost soul that I was. Eventually, I returned to England.

I rented a terraced house in Wombwell, near Barnsley. I found unsatisfactory employment in a meat packaging factory, the name of which I have gratefully erased from my memory.

I had always liked Knaresborough, North Yorkshire, and decided to move there. It was whilst in Knaresborough that I learned of the death of a boyhood friend of mine, Tommy.

Tommy and I were extremely close. We went to the same school and joined the Army Cadets together. From what I could gather, he had died of a heart attack whilst on a walking holiday in Wales. He must only have been fifty nine years old.

I remembered the last time I saw him; I was at my Mothers' place in Grimethorpe. I had my head under the bonnet of my car and when I withdrew it, I saw Tommy walking down the street with his back to me. He must have passed me without realising it. By now, he was about fifty yards from me and I did consider running after him to say hello. Now, I truly regret not doing so.

Tommy's funeral had taken place prior to me finding out about his death. So, I thought the least I could do was put some flowers on his grave. So, I drove the thirty seven or so miles to Grimethorpe to seek out his grave, in the small cemetery there. It was a bitterly cold day, and wrapped up in my overcoat, I systematically searched for his headstone, but I just couldn't find it. I found the grave his parents shared but not Tommy's. I had been assured that he had been buried, as opposed to cremated, so it was a mystery. Unlikely as it seemed, he must have been buried elsewhere. I placed the flowers on his parents' grave; they had always been good to me; and drove home. That night, I was reading by a bedside lamp, and feeling a shift in the air, I looked up and there was Tommy. He looked really young, almost like a teenager. He was smiling at me and he said, "I know you have been looking for me." Now when I say he spoke to me, what I heard was his voice inside my head.

Only twice have spirits spoken to me and both of the spirits were of people I had known in life. Tommy went on to tell me where his headstone was. A few days later, armed with more flowers, I entered the cemetery and walked straight to his grave.

What had thrown me was that Tommy's son had died young and Tommy had been buried with him. I had looked at this headstone, but on seeing his sons' name, I had looked no further. Had I read the full inscription, I would have seen Tommy's name under his sons', and saved Tommy a journey. Still, it was nice to see him again.

Thank you, Tommy; a friend to the end.

*****

Having failed my Eleven Plus, I was enrolled at Brierley Secondary Modern School. As the name suggests, it was a modern building with a gym and playing fields.

The grading there was A, B, C, and D. I must have done reasonably well in my Eleven Plus because I was graded as a 'C'. Explaining to my Mother that I had graduated to just "being thick," she asked for a second opinion.

On my final exam at this school, I was to finish third in the 'A Stream'. My Mother accused me of falsifying my school report and sent it off for forensics.

*****

My very best friend at school was the previously mentioned, Tommy - we gelled from day one. He was such a nice lad with a cheeky smile and a generous nature. We spent all our free time together roaming the woods and building dens, along with the ever-present Rex.

Another two lads that would sometimes join us were Alan and Michael. Alan was a little younger than us, but he had an amazing way with animals; he had an affinity with them and they with him. He didn't mollycoddle them and treat them like pets. He could be quite harsh with them, but never cruel. He would go ferreting for rabbits, and on removing them from the nets, would think nothing of snapping their necks in one, quick action. Whereas, myself and Tommy would be a bit squeamish. Alan would just roll his eyes and say, "Give it here!"

Sometimes, we would raid the backyard of the Ex-Servicemens Club, 'The Bullet'. The Club kept all of their empty beer bottles, and best of all, empty soda siphons there. The bottles had a threepence returnable fee on them, but the soda siphons had a whopping two shillings and sixpence back on them. So, if available, the siphons were our goal. I suppose this was stealing, but we preferred to call it 'recycling'.

The problem was that they kept a big Alsatian in the yard, to deter little sods, such as us, from thieving. So, Alan, Tommy and I, would take it in turns to brave the dog. One of us would be hoisted up to look over the high fence and check if the dog was about. If not, over he would go, grab the bottles, and then throw them over the fence into the waiting arms of his mates.

One day, having checked that the coast was clear, over I went. Feeling pleased with myself, I began tossing the bottles over to Alan and Tommy. Suddenly, from nowhere, I heard this very low growl. Slowly turning my head, I saw this great big bloody Alsatian sitting behind me with its teeth bared. I could feel the blood drain from my face. Well normally, you would have to pile a couple of crates up against the fence to get back over it. I didn't need them! I don't know how I did it, but in one leap, I was astride the fence and over. On doing this, I could hear gales of laughter coming from the Clubs open window; they must have seen me and let the dog out.

Collapsing at the other side of the fence, I was astonished to see Alan and Tommy rolling about laughing. It was a few days before I could see the funny side of it.

*****

Staying with Alan for awhile… One day I was up in the woods with him. Alan, who was always the bravest of our gang, had climbed to the top of a silver birch tree and was crawling along a very thin branch. I shouted up to him to come down as the branch was beginning to bend. Sure enough, the branch snapped, and down came Alan. Surrounding this tree was a series of jagged tree stumps and Alan's leg became impaled on one. A sliver of wood protruding from a stump had gone right through his calf, amazingly missing the bone. There was little or no blood and Alan very calmly said, "Don't just stand there, lift me off!" Feeling a little faint, I put my arms under him and in one mighty heave, lifted him off the stump. He never flinched.

We were both calm and in control. Then, Alan looked down at his leg and said, "OH! NO! My giblets are coming out!" Well, I didn't know what giblets were; I still don't, but it sounded pretty horrific to me. "OH! NO! Not your giblets!" I cried. What Alan had seen was the fatty tissue poking out from his wound. Now we were both panicking… "Stay calm!" I screamed, running around like a headless chicken.

I then noticed a pram ('stroller') in the back garden of a house adjoining the wood. Grabbing hold of it (and without the owner's permission), I bundled Alan into it. Luckily, the return journey was all downhill. Seconds later, I was charging down Cemetery Hill with Alan in the pushchair flopping about like a bloody Guy Fawkes.

Spilling to a halt outside Dad's shop, I ran in and said "Dad, it's my mate, Alan - his giblets are coming out!" Muttering something along the lines of "Why me?" Dad drove Alan to the hospital and stitches were inserted. (I don't know what they did with the giblets…)

Back at school the next day, all the lads were saying, "Hey, Gordon, your mate, Alan, 'as had an accident."
"I know," I said importantly, "I was there. his giblets were coming out!"
"Oh, no! Not his giblets!" They all chorused. The dozy gits didn't know what giblets were either…!

*****

Michael was sort of on the fringes of our little gang. A red-haired, gangling lad, who lived at the bottom of what was once a park. He was a really nice lad who loved his music, but he lacked the ability to stand up for himself.

During the really bad winter of 1962 to 63, I called on him so that we could walk to school together. (It really was a horrendous winter - absolutely freezing. How I managed my paper round that winter, I will never know…riding a bike was out of the question!) I arrived at Michaels' to find him in tears. He had a pet rabbit in a hutch in the backyard. The hutch was well insulated with a heavy rug thrown over it and that should have protected his rabbit, Snowy.

Alas, Snowy was frozen solid, stretched out as stiff as a board. "It's Snowy!" wailed Michael. "He's deed! He's deed!" Then, to my amazement, he grabbed Snowy by the hind legs and started smashing his head against the hutch, as if to prove his point. *Clunk! Clunk! Clunk!* "He's deed!

He's deed!" again, wailed Michael. I thought, well if he wasn't dead before, he is now! "Err…perhaps if you leave him in front of the fire for a bit…?" I suggested limply.

*****

One Christmas, I did a silly thing; it's funny how kids can be so sensitive. We were given a little envelope by the school for donations to a charity for the blind. I can see the picture on the envelope now: a little, blonde haired girl, looking up with sightless eyes into a golden light. I took the envelope home and Dad put two old pennies into it. I knew that a lot of my classmates' parents would put six pennies into their envelope - not a sixpenny piece, but six pennies to bulk it up.

I was ashamed that my envelope would look so thin in comparison, so I removed the two pennies, burnt the envelope, and told the teacher I had forgotten it. As the other kids queued up to give their donations, I just sat there red faced.

I had no intention of keeping the money, so I sneaked into the larder where my Mother kept her purse. I was just putting the coins into her purse when she caught me. Of course, she thought that I was taking the coins out of her purse. What could I say…? I was ashamed to take such a small donation to school, so the charity ended up with nothing? I was branded a thief and given a clout. Also, I was shamed at school for not returning my envelope. What was I thinking?

The moral of the story is this: if you are going to be stupid, at least keep the two pennies!

*****

It was nearing Christmas and the school gave its pupils a choice. For the last period of the afternoon, they could either watch the school team playing football or sing carols in the Hall. Of course, most of the boys, including myself and Tommy, opted to watch football. The girls chose to sing carols in the Hall.

It was a freezing cold afternoon, and at half-time, I suggested to Tommy that we sneaked off home. We got caught by a teacher and marched in front of the Headmaster. I shall call him Dobbs.

Dobbs was a small, portly man, who was never seen to smile. He was very abrupt and you could have been forgiven for believing that he hated kids. He was despised by the pupils and I suspect that he was disliked by many of the teachers, too. I was not surprised when he ordered us onto the stage to be caned in front of a Hall full of girls. I accept what we did was wrong and that we should have been punished, but it should have been done privately.

To his credit, the teacher that caught us (a nice man), looked embarrassed and hung his head. He seemed surprised at the action Dobbs was taking. We laid no blame on him.

It was to be three strokes on each hand and if you withdrew your hand, which is a natural thing to do, you received an extra stroke. The Headmaster, making a big play of it in front of the girls, lined up my hand and brought the cane down three times. Hitting me, not on the hand, but on the ends of my cold fingers. Each time he struck, he gave a little jump, to ensure his full weight was behind the blow.

Then the other hand received the same treatment. Whilst he was caning me, I looked him straight in the eyes with a little smile on my face. Probably not a wise thing to do as his face was getting redder and redder…but I wanted him to know that I had 'sussed him out' and knew what a sadistic, little bastard he was.

I felt bad when it was Tommy's turn, as I had got him into this trouble. But Tommy being Tommy, never threw any blame my way.

After punishing us, I half expected Dobbs to bow to the audience. Fortunately, we had the weekend off and the swelling had gone down by Monday.

Many of the teaching staff had served during the War. I often wondered if Dobbs had been one of them, and maybe the War had affected him somehow.

Tommy and I now planned our revenge on Dobbs… We considered garrotting him then decapitation. But, as we didn't know what those words meant, we settled on the old 'spud in the car exhaust' routine. The theory being that you jam a spud into the exhaust pipe of a car, then, when the engine is revved, the pressure in the exhaust builds up and this propels the spud from the exhaust with a loud bang. Brilliant, eh?

The day came and I sneaked into the school car park and stuck a spud into Dobbs' exhaust pipe. We waited patiently, hiding behind a small wall. Dobbs eventually got into his car and revved the engine. We watched with just our eyes showing above the wall. We must have looked like a couple of 'Kilroy's'.

Sniggering in anticipation, we heard a terrific *bang!* then looked… Where did the spud go? The car seemed to shudder for a while, and then the whole of the exhaust system dropped off. We looked at each other in horror before crawling off faster than most people can run. Once clear of the small wall, we stood and ran for our lives. I swear that we were followed by a sonic boom!

*****

It was whilst at school that I joined the Army Cadets, along with Tommy. The Cadets were based in South Kirby, which was a village about a half hours bus ride from Grimethorpe. It was basically just a hut, and even at full strength, we numbered about twelve. It was run by a Mr Miller, an ex-soldier, who kindly gave up his spare time to tutor us in the art of soldiering. We were issued with battledress and, for a small weekly membership fee, we could pretend to be soldiers, though I believe we had to buy our own boots, which was understandable.

We went on an annual camp, usually under canvas somewhere in Cumbria. Once a year, we also attended the Territorial Army's Indoor .22 Shooting Range in Wakefield. This was to qualify for our marksmanship badges.

One evening, we were joined by an ex-Cadet, who was now a serving soldier. This young man appeared in uniform and spoke to us at some length on what it was like to serve as a 'regular' soldier. He regaled us with talk of his many adventures, but not in a boastful way. I was enthralled by what he had to say and looked at him in his smart uniform with admiration. I noticed his cap badge that showed a French hunting horn, which sat neatly on his green beret. I wasn't to know it then, but this meeting would influence a decision I was to make in the near future…

*****

Finally, aged fifteen, my time at Brierley Secondary Modern School came to an end, and I was interviewed by the School's Careers Officer; a rather dour man who didn't seem interested in what I wanted to do but in what he wanted me to do, and that was go down the pit.

I explained with some patience that I wanted to be a lighthouse keeper. He looked at me with some confusion, and then with equal patience, explained to me that there was not a great demand for lighthouse keepers in Barnsley. Primarily because it was fifty miles from the coast. He had a point!

"Out of interest…" he said, "Why do you want to be a lighthouse keeper?"
"I like reading," I explained, "And it seems to me that all a lighthouse keeper has to do is top up the oil for the lamp every couple of weeks giving him plenty of time to read."
This was followed by a long silence.
"Yes," he replied, "but have you considered that you would have to walk around in circles in order to read your book?"
It would be some days before I was to realise the meaning of this joke. Maybe he was not as dour as I thought.
"Well can I be a shepherd then?" I asked hopefully.

*****

Three weeks later, I found myself in the pit offices, waiting to be interviewed. I had not applied to work at Grimethorpe Colliery, I had simply received a letter asking me to attend an interview. Obviously, there wasn't a great demand for shepherds in Barnsley either, and the Careers Officer had forwarded my name. A portly man in a flat cap interviewed me, if you can call it that? He was the spitting image of the character, Albert Tatlock, from the early series of Coronation Street.

"So, tha' wants t' work down't pit does tha'?"

I was unsure on how to answer this, but I would have looked an idiot if I had said no.

"Yes," I answered, with little enthusiasm.
"Reet, sign theer'," he said, handing me a piece of paper. And that was it. That was the interview. Christ, I thought, they must be desperate! So, I signed "theer' " as instructed, and then he shouted, making me jump…
"What's tha' just signed?"
Confused, I said, "to work down't pit?"
"Tha' dun't know what tha's signed - tha' ne'er read it. Ne'er sign owt wi'out readin' it!"
Since that day, I never have!

*****

After a few months training, which involved a few weeks at Hemsworth Technical College and underground training at Ferrymoor Colliery, I was put to work on the screens at Grimethorpe. It was illegal for lads to work underground until they reached the age of sixteen. This excluded going underground at Ferrymoor because that was training not working. So, I had about eight months to work on the pit top before my sixteenth birthday.

The screens consisted of a conveyor belt that ran along a high gantry. This gantry was covered with corrugated sheeting which offered little protection from the elements. Then again, it couldn't be too enclosed because clouds of coal dust would rise up from the conveyor belt as coal was dropped down a chute onto it. Ventilation was needed to disperse the dust.

Along with two or three other lads, I would drag these huge lumps of coal to one side and they would go down a chute into a wagon on a railway siding. If memory serves me right, I think that we were expected to fill seven wagons in this manner during the course of a shift.

I actually went down the pit on my sixteenth birthday. I soon became acclimatised to the conditions and enjoyed the camaraderie that existed amongst men and women that work in dangerous environments.

I worked on the haulage with two other lads, Mick and Nev. Our job was to haul supplies up to the headings. Starting at the pit bottom, we would be given seven or eight trams loaded up with pit props, steel girders (rings), bagging, rubber belting, and anything else that was required. We would then begin our long journey up to the headings, dropping off supplies where needed.

I think we supplied four or five headings. The trams were hauled on an endless steel rope that we fastened to the trams by means of a clamp (clip). A signal would start the rope moving and the trams would be hauled along on rails. Having serviced our last heading, we returned to the pit bottom with the empty trams. This would bring us to the end of our eight hour shift, when all we had left to do was wait for the cage to return us to the surface when the shift ended.

Of course, it was never as simple as that. We would have derailments, worn clamps, we would jump and slip on the steel rope causing the trams to break loose; no two days were the same.

However, I liked the job. As long as you did your work, you would be left alone; you could organise your own day, there were no set times for having your 'snap' (packed lunch), you would have your 'snap' whenever and wherever you could. Officially, you were allowed twenty minutes during the working day, but the Deputies didn't mind as long as the job was done, and it always was. Even if you could only manage ten minutes for your 'snap', it was all based on trust. Even sixteen year olds like us were treated like adults.

It angers me when people say miners were overpaid, something that was often said during the Miners' Strike of the 1980s. Consider this. They worked in a hostile environment, subject to roof falls, gas, and the biggest killer of them all, dust. Coal dust killed more miners than anything else. The miners called it 'Black Lung'. The doctors called it Pneumoconiosis.

The deprivation miners endured were these: they were not issued with masks in those days; obviously, they were unable to smoke because of the gas and risk of explosions; there was no clean water supply down the pit - you had to carry your own water in a canteen and when it was gone, it was gone; no access to hot food, despite often working in cold, wet conditions; even the basic needs were not catered for - not even toilets - if you wanted a shit, you literally had to shit on a shovel and then throw it onto the conveyor belt (the shit, not the shovel) – sorry about the use of the word "shit", but I can't spell "excrement".

I was paid £6 a week, and having paid Mum for my board and lodging, I was left with thirty bob (£1.50). So, you can see that we were not, by any means, paid a fortune. But the money was just about enough for me to get by on.

*****

Now I was earning some money, I was able to buy some decent clothes. In those days, a girl wouldn't go out with you unless you dressed smartly. So, I was straight off to Burtons for an off-the-peg suit. More clothes were bought with the aid of Littlewood's catalogue. A lovely 'deaf and dumb' lady called Phyllis Littlewood was their local agent, and my first purchase was a pair of 'Winkle Pickers', which were a type of very pointy, long-toed shoe.

My brother, Kevin, would soon have my gear away if I didn't watch him - the little sod! He still douses himself in my expensive aftershave on visits to my home even now. I have got to hide the stuff! He leaves my cheap stuff alone. Still, it shows he has taste. (You didn't know I knew, did you, Kev?)

The pub landlords had a sensible approach to underage drinking at the time, particularly the local ones. Their attitude was, if you are old enough to work down the pit, then you are old enough to drink.

Of course, they didn't take your word for it, they would quiz you. "What seam do you work on? Who is your Deputy?" They trusted you to know when you had drunk enough beer and we never let them down. They treated us like adults, so we behaved like adults. I started drinking aged sixteen.

There were three Working Men's Clubs in Grimethorpe and one pub called The Grimethorpe Hotel, known affectionately as the 'Top Boozer'. Sadly, it has been pulled down, as have many pubs. There used to be some great pubs in Barnsley. To my knowledge, there are only Chennels, The Corner Pin, and the Old No.7 left from the sixties.

*****

I was now three months short of my eighteenth birthday.

I had been at the pit for nearly three years, during which time I was seeing a girl called Jane, and for reasons that were never explained, she finished with me. I was no longer looking at the stars and dreaming of travel and adventures. In fact, where I was working I couldn't even see the stars. Something had to change.

On the 14th of September, 1965, I walked into the Army Recruiting Office in Barnsley and asked to join the Navy.

"This is an Army Recruiting Office," the Recruiting Sergeant said.

"Oh, I know!" I replied, "I was hoping you could tell me where to go?"

"Well, it's Crown House in Sheffield," sighed the Sergeant. "What's wrong with the Army?"

I wanted to travel, I explained.

"You will travel in the Infantry," he persisted. I was about to thank him and leave when I noticed his cap badge. A French hunting horn on a green beret; a similar badge to the one that the young soldier had worn all those years ago in the Cadet hut.

"What are you in?" I asked.

"The Kings Own Yorkshire Light Infantry," he proudly said.

Two weeks later, I was boarding a steam train to Sir John Moore's Barracks, Shrewsbury, Shropshire, via Birmingham. I had never been on a train before. As the train clattered out of Barnsley Station, a deluge of memories engulfed me, and my past shouted after me like a stirring of echoes.

The Battle of Woolley Edge

The laughter of children clings to the air
with shouts of " I will, who dare?"
Large leafy trees which look down and smile;
these children are ours at least for a while.

Fairy book dragons appear in the haze,
with ember red eyes and feet made of clays.
We unsheathe our swords of stick, twig and fern -
these monsters of myth must die in their turn.

We thrust and we hack at peppermint backs,
through marshmallows tails and wings made of sails.
Brother Steve, brother Stew both fought well and slew,
these creatures where part of the stories they knew.

Honour gained, the ground is stained with honey and dew,
we make our way back through forests of yew.
Waist coated toads on paper laced roads,
dance out a tune to the beat of a spoon.

Roy Rogers, Gene Autrey and Jim Bowie too,
greet us aloud as we step off a cloud;
their faces are kind and their thoughts throw no spears,
these heroes of old from comic books sold.

"Gordon, Stewart, Steven", they call,
"Quick to the car you have wandered too far,"
"Your faces are dirty, your hands and your clothes,"
"Please stop your snivelling and do blow your nose".

Once dragons, now logs and toads become frogs,
that laugh at our youth as we learn of the truth,
Our heroes are celluloid, remember the tales?
From days in the pictures on bottle back sales.

Though worry and hardship are banners of old,
our parents did cry out as magic was sold.
They see not our armour but hand me down clothes,
Our shoes needed mending because of the snows.

Great battles at Woolley we no longer fight,
since dreams in our manhood are restricted to night;
killed by knowledge and leaning our magic did die:
And love, truth and friendship replaced by the lie.

Old ghosts there still wander from holly to rock,
in search of eight children that time had forgot.
Their laughter now echoes that winds can't erase,
small shadows still chase through deep purples and greys.

These children, now grown up and scattered like seeds,
who bend to their worries like snow laden reeds,
The distance is short from sharp twig to sharp tongue,
from pure laughter to scorn, from nightfall to dawn.

So, follow your children when fantasy reigns
and soar with dark ravens through valley and plains.
Remember my warning for all of our sakes,
for the battle of Woolley is fought in our wakes.

Footnote

Woolley is a small mining village on the outskirts of Barnsley. On the edge of the village lies a small wooded area set amongst rocky outcrops. For eight children living in the far larger community of Grimethorpe, visits to Woolley always provided us with an oasis of magic, in an area sadly ravaged by heavy industry.

The Waster

Robert Winston was a waster, as simple as that. Twenty four years old, and reportedly, had only worked one week in his entire life. On leaving school, he had completed one week of the six weeks training that the pit demanded a lad must complete, before being allowed to work underground. He left, vowing that he would never work down that bloody hole again. Work!? It wasn't even work, it was instruction.

Winston possessed that easy charm that most wasters seem to have. Always ready with a joke and a great slapper of backs.

His slight frame haunted the bookies, pubs and Working Men's Clubs in the mining village of Tollthorpe. He never had any money, yet was always playing the Bandits, placing bets, and could always be found with a pint in his hand. He was forever on the cadge: "Got a ciggie, mate? Just about to buy you a pint, pal, but I seem to have run out of money. You will? Oh, cheers. Get you one back later. Have you got a 'bob' for the Bandit? It's about to drop. Pay you back out of the winnings." Winston's easy smile and good nature usually brought results, leaving his victims ruefully shaking their heads at their own folly.

Robert Winston was a waster, as simple as that.

In contrast, Tommy Fletcher was forty years old, a hard worker, well respected, a solid husband and father. In other words, everything that Winston was not.

Fletcher had worked at Tollthorpe Colliery for twenty five years, leaving school at fifteen, to work on the underground haulage before going on to work on the coal face. Of medium height and build, he was a good looking man in a rugged sort of way. He was not known for his sense of humour but well respected and liked.

Tollthorpe was a thriving village in the sixties. It was one of many pit villages orbiting Barnsley, with plenty of shops, pubs and clubs to provide entertainment and drink for the thirsty miners. People in general had money in their pockets, though not as much as many people thought. Although miners earned a decent wage, it was only the face workers that earned the big money; they were able to enhance their basic wage with productivity bonuses when possible.

*****

Tommy Fletcher had first met Mavis Clinton on a Club coach outing to Blackpool. They had been seated together on the coach and got talking. He had recently celebrated his twentieth birthday; Mavis was two years his junior. She lived in a neighbouring village and he was instantly attracted to her. She was not beautiful in the conventional sense, but she was pretty with intelligent, brown eyes and a neat figure. He was enchanted by her shyness, sensing a capability and strength about her.

Tom's Mothers' voice echoed back through the years, "When tha' marries, lad, marry a lass that's careful. Looks aren't everything. It's careful and common sense that's important!" Tom wasn't sure what his mother meant by "careful", but he reckoned Mavis was. A year later, Tom and Mavis were married in Saint Luke's, the local village church.

Tom and his wife were granted a pit house. A terrace, back-to-back, a short walk from the pit head. Things were tight at first, but bit-by-bit, they managed to put a cosy home together. Mavis absolutely refused to buy on credit. So, they often had to make do with second-hand things until they could be replaced by new.

All-in-all they were very happy together, and their happiness was complete with the arrival of their baby daughter, two years later. Secretly, Tom had wanted a son, but one look at little Joan, and he was smitten. He drove his wife crazy checking on the baby every two minutes, and would fly into a panic every time she cried. Mavis would often plead with Tom's best friend, Lenny, "For God's sake, take that man down to the pub for a few hours. He is driving me nuts!"

Of course, things settled and Tom delighted in watching Joan grow. He would swing her onto his shoulders and take her down to his allotment and show her how to plant vegetables and flowers. The faces she pulled when eating the sour tasting gooseberries sent him into gales of laughter. She was Daddy's little girl.

The years passed, and Joan, now a teenager, no longer ran squealing into his arms when he came home from work, nor demanded to go down to the allotment to make flowers and feed the "Chuckies." No more the feel of her little hand sliding into his jacket pocket, in search of the chocolate biscuit that Mavis put in with his work sandwiches that he always saved for her. Now it was all Beatles, boys and mini-skirts. But she was still very much Daddy's little girl.

Like most miners in those days, Tom handed his wage packet over to his wife on the Friday, after taking out the agreed amount of pocket money for his beer and pipe tobacco. He always made sure that she was not left short of housekeeping money, unlike some miners who took a larger portion of pocket money leaving their wives short, and yet still expected meat with every meal.

They had long since settled into a routine. Mavis was thrifty, kept the house spotless, provided excellent meals and was a good mother to Joan. In turn, Tom never missed a shift even when unwell, worked his allotment providing the larder with fresh vegetables, fruit and eggs. He was not heavy on the beer and saw to it that Mavis shared his leisure time on a weekend. Their love life may not have been what it was, but that was only to be expected after twenty years of marriage. In short, they made a good team.

*****

"Come on, love, Lenny and Pat are saving us a seat."
"Give me a minute. I've laddered me stockings!"
Saturday night was the night wives and girlfriends joined
the men for a night out. This usually meant 'The Club'.
There were three clubs in the village. Everyone had their
favourite, but it was usually what turns or acts were
showing that night that decided which one was attended.

"Where are we going?" Mavis's voice floated down the
stairs.
"'Stute." This was short for 'Miners' Institute'.
"Who's on?"
"Bloody Frank Sinatra. Come on, woman."
"Who?"
Holding his head in his hands, "A lass that sings like Dusty
Springfield and a comedian a bit like me."
"Oh! I thought you said it was Frank Sinatra."

Arm in arm, they walked down the street. He could not
help but noticing how pretty his wife was when she was
dressed up. A little thicker around the waist, but still a
looker. He had often wondered why they had not had any
more children - it had just not happened; not that it had
bothered either of them. They were happy with Joan.

As promised, Lenny and Pat had saved them seats in the
crowded Club. Lenny was a little leprechaun of a man with
a cheeky smile; nothing seemed to faze him. Pat was a
stout, bottle blonde, with an infectious laugh.

Halfway through the night, they came round with the Bingo tickets. Tom couldn't stand the game, but Mavis took it very seriously. Strange; she couldn't abide gambling, but never considered Bingo as gambling. For himself, the weekly football pools were as far as he went.

He was on his fifth pint and Mavis on her third Babycham when the last card had been marked, "I only wanted three numbers!" chimed Mavis. Tom and Lenny shared a smile. Tom was packing his pipe when he felt a presence at his shoulder, and the skinny, unwashed form of Robert Winston loomed over him.

"'Ow do, Mr Fletcher, Missus? Tha' ain't got five bob I can borrow fort' pool table as tha'? 'Cause I ain't got no change tha' sees."

"Plenty of change behind bar." Replied Tom in disgust.

"Aye, I know, but there's a queue at bar like."

"Don't mind him, love. Here you are," interrupted Mavis, going into her purse.

"Thanks, Mrs Fletcher," said Winston, flashing his rotten teeth.

"I'll see you get it back!"

"If we're not in, just put it through the letter box," snarled Tom.

"Yeah, reet," Winston nodded, the sarcasm going right over his head.

"How's your Joan, Mrs Fletcher?"

"She's fine, Robert. Works in't' baker's shop on the High Street. You know, Mayhews? Been there a year now. She's eighteen next month."
"Aye, thought I saw her there. Bonny lass. Any road, thanks fort' money."

If it had not been for Lenny grabbing hold of his arm, Tom would have strangled Winston there and then. The thought that his daughters' name had even been mentioned by that fox-faced lump of shit, turned his stomach. The night was ruined.

On returning home, all thoughts of love making were forgotten. Tom went straight to bed, ignoring Mavis's query of "something wrong, love?"

*****

Monday morning saw Tom and Mavis in their cosy kitchen; it was 5am and the early shift beckoned. His wife had always insisted on getting up with him, despite his protests.

"There's no need, love, just put me snap (sandwiches) up night before."
"I like to get up and make you a bit of breakfast, even if it is only a slice of toast," she replied. "Anyway, your snap will stay fresher if it's made up in in't' morning."

He never really understood the logic of this. But then, what Tom didn't know, was the real reason his wife insisted on seeing him off in the morning, was the thought that it might be the last time she would see him alive.

A tap on the window heralded Lenny's arrival at the house; they always walked to work together.

"Thought tha' was going to batter that Winston lad Saturday neet."
"Our lass still thinks I am mad over t'five bob. She can't see I don't want that bloke anywhere near our Joan," sighed Tom.
Lenny scratched his head, "I don't know what tha's worried about. Your Joan wouldn't look twice at a bloke like that."
"Aye, happen your reet," nodded Tom.

*****

"Where you off to then?" Joan was making for the door, all dressed up.
"Just going to the pictures with Ann and Mary, Dad."
"Have you considered putting some clothes on?"
"Everyone's wearing mini-skirts now, Dad!" Joan giggled.
"I'm not!" replied Tom. "Any road, what's on? Better not be an X-rated film?"
"Hey, I am eighteen and old enough to watch them now. But it's not an X-rated film. I think it's a Jerry Lewis film," said Joan, throwing her Dad a kiss and opening the door.
"Hey, wait a minute…teck this." Tom's hand held a ten shilling note.
"Ah…Dad. Thanks!" His reward was a kiss on the forehead.

She was still Daddy's little girl.

*****

"Don't see much of Joan these days. She's always out." Tom, looking up from his Pools coupon, addressed his wife. Mavis just grunted.

"I said…" began Tom.

"I heard you!" snapped Mavis.

"Well, you might as well know; you'll find out anyway," began Mavis, "She's courting!"

"Nowt wrong with that, she's eighteen. Who is it?" The room filled with silence. "Mavis, who is it?" He pushed his chair back, held his wife by the shoulders, and demanded, "For the last time, who is it?"

"Robert Winston!" She cried, pushing him away. Tom stared at her for a few seconds, then a grin spread across his face.

"No, seriously, love, who is it?"

*****

The weeks that followed were a nightmare. His initial reaction was to find Winston and warn him off. If you do that, his wife cautioned, you will lose your daughter. "I have already lost my daughter!" was his response.

He had tried calmly talking to Joan, taking her down to the allotment as he had done when she was a little kid, making them a cup of tea with the old primus stove he kept in the shed.

"Reet, love, I am not here to upset thee or argue with thee. Just help me to understand what tha' sees in that Winston bloke."

"For a start, his name is Robert. He makes me laugh and he's nice to me. He's not as bad as folk make out. He'd get a job but it's his asthma. He's not like other people," said Joan, wringing her hands nervously.

"Bloody right he's not like other people, and as for his asthma, he took a pit medical before he began his training. If he had asthma, they wouldn't have allowed him to start training in the first place, not even for the one week he managed to complete." He had not meant to raise his voice, but he had.

"I knew you wouldn't understand. It's hopeless trying to reason with you!" cried Joan, and with that, she ran from the allotment.

Tom sat with his head in his hands. She was no longer Daddy's little girl.

*****

During the days that followed, an uneasy truce prevailed between Tom and Joan. They were polite to each other, but unable to hold each other's eyes. Mavis fluttered around them like a referee in a boxing match. Joan spent most of her time in her room. "It's like living with two ghosts!" sobbed Mavis.

Tom's mates noticed the change in him, and knowing the cause, never mentioned either Joan or Winston in his company. Mavis was right; he walked around like a ghost.

Lenny took him for a pint one Friday night to the Colliers Arms. He knew Winston wouldn't be there; he was staying well away from Tom. Robert Winston was now doing his drinking in Lumpton - a small village, three miles from Tollthorpe, where his parents lived.

Lenny put two pints on the table. He had noticed his friend was drinking more these days.

"OK, mate?" Lenny enquired.

"Aye, fine, Lenny."
"Look, Tom, all your mates are worried about you. Don't you think you are tecking this Winston thing too seriously?"
"Yeah, I bet you are having a right laugh behind me back!" sneered Tom.
"Now you know it's not like that," said Lenny, sharply.
"If you'll teck my advice…" began Lenny.
"Your advice?! Your advice?! You're the one that said Joan wouldn't go anywhere near the bastard!"
Lenny's little leprechaun face crumpled up in anguish.
"Aye, happen your reet, Tom. I'm not good at giving advice and judging folk. After all, I married our Pat."

Tom couldn't help but smile into his beer at his friends' misery.

*****

The day started bad and got a whole lot worse. He had arrived at his allotment to find that a fox had got in with his chickens. He returned home in a bad mood to find Mavis standing before him with her arms folded. "Reet, Tom. Let's get it over with… Joan's just told me that she is going to marry Robert!" His response was quick and short. "I want her out of this house!" Slamming the door, he left for the pub.

The next Mavis saw of Tom was when Lenny brought him home in a taxi at midnight. She had never seen her husband drunk before…merry, yes, but never drunk! Another thing she had never seen before was Tom not getting up for his morning shift the next day.

Initially, on hearing about the wedding, Tom had thought that Joan was pregnant. He simply couldn't believe that anyone would want to marry *that* waster, Winston, unless they felt that they had to. Taking her to one side, he explained to her that she didn't have to get married; that both he and her Mum would help her with the baby at home.

"What baby?" Joan asked incredulously. Then slowly, her eyes widened, and she slapped his face.

As the day of the wedding drew near, Tom was adamant that he wouldn't be going. Mavis begged him to relent, if not for Joan's sake, then for hers.

All their married life, they had rarely argued. But the days leading up to the wedding were filled with accusations, threats and tears. When Mavis threatened to leave him, he finally relented.

The wedding was held at Barnsley Registry Office on a cold, March morning. The reception was to be held at Tom's Club in Tollthorpe. He had paid for a large buffet and put a generous amount of money behind the bar for drinks.

Back at the reception, Joan looked radiant in a white wedding dress that Tom had paid for. Robert Winston looked a mess in a shoddy, badly stained, blue suit that Tom had not paid for.

Tom and Mavis were introduced to his parents. The father, a weasel of a man, was strutting about in a suit three sizes too big for him, trying to give the impression that he had paid for everything. The mother was a mousey looking woman. She looked care worn and cowed, and Tom felt a stab of sympathy for her. When she returned his smile, she gave him a look that said, "Now you can see what I have to put up with?"

He had promised Mavis that he would behave himself and he had kept that promise, but that didn't stop her from shadowing his every move. He told his daughter that he was sorry, how much he loved her and that she was still his little girl. She hugged her Dad and choked back the tears. Mavis thanked him with a loving smile. The only thing he held back on was the speech; that would have been too much.

Robert Winston was never away from the bar, making sure that himself, and his family and friends, had plenty of drink before the money ran out.

Things were going relatively well until the evening neared its end. Tom was using the urinal in the gents, when suddenly the door burst open, and in staggered a drunken Robert Winston, "'Ow do, Dad?" he slurred with a smirk on his face. The speed in which Tom moved surprised them both. Grabbing Winston by the throat, he bundled him into a cubicle and locked the door. "Tha's always got to push tha' luck 'asn't tha'?" snarled Tom, tightening his grip on Winston's throat. "Now listen to me, if you ever call me Dad again, if you ever hurt Joan, or if you ever go near my home, I promise you I will kill you… You are nothing but a waster…!" And with that, he drove his fist into Winston's stomach.

Leaving his son-in-law curled up on the cubicle floor, he made his way back to the reception. "Everything alright?" queried Mavis. "Couldn't be better, love!" he said, taking his wife's hand and leading her to the dance floor.

*****

After the wedding, Joan and Winston had rented a flat in Lumpton. Joan still worked at the baker's shop and he knew that she was visiting her Mum whilst he was out of the house. He also knew that Mavis was giving her money. He didn't mind any of these things, but what narked him was that they felt that they had to keep it a secret from him.

The following winter had been the worst in living memory, and February saw the worst of it. The snow was ankle deep and public transport badly affected.

Tom entered the Colliers Arms followed by flurry of snow. He noticed Lenny and Terry Coyle deep in conversation at a corner table. They had not seen him come in and looked up in surprise when he put his pint on the table and joined them. "Alreet, lads?" he offered. They both looked very shifty.

"OK! What is it?" Tom glared at Lenny.
"Nowt, Tom, honest!" Lenny countered.
"Oh, for God's sake! I'll tell him! He's a right to know!" This came from Terry.
"Know what?" said Tom.
"It's your Joan's husband, that Winston lad. He's been playing around with that redhead that lives on Brighton Street. The one with three kids, whose husband left her. What's her name?"
"Betty Stokes…" volunteered Lenny.
"Aye, Betty Stokes, that's her…" continued Terry.
"What!? The little bastard has only been married eleven months and Betty Stokes must be in her forties!" exploded Tom.
"Well, it seems that he was seeing her before he married your Joan. There has been talk of others as well, but I don't

know about that." Terry mumbled, beginning to wish he was elsewhere.

"Now, let's get this straight!" Tom shouted, causing heads to turn. "Just how sure are you of this, Terry?"

"Well…" began Terry, "I have seen them together three or four times in Barnsley. They go there in the hope that they won't be spotted."

Tom's face turned ashen. "I warned him! I warned that little shit bag! I am going to bloody well…"

Tom stopped mid-sentence. Slowly, a beatific smile lit his face, followed by a laugh. Lenny and Terry looked at each other in alarm, then they both stared at Tom, mouths agape.

"You…you…you alreet, Tom?" stuttered Lenny.

"Never better, Lenny…never better! Don't you see? When Joan finds out about this, and I'll make sure that she does, she'll either throw him out, or better still, come back home to live with us. Either way, we are rid of the waster!"

When Tom returned home, Mavis was at the sink washing dishes. "You're home early!" she said. He noticed for the first time that her hair was dusted with grey. She looked tired and he felt a surge of love for her.

"Missed my wife, haven't I?" he said, putting his arms around her waist and kissing her neck.

"Bloody Hell!" she exclaimed, "Beer must be strong tonight!"

"Sit down, lass, we need to talk," he replied, pulling a chair out for her.

"What's up?" she said, alarmed.

"Well, it's about Winston. He's been…"

"I know!" snapped Mavis.

"You KNOW!?" He looked at her like he had never seen her before.

"If you are referring to that Stokes woman…? I know!"

"Well, lass, don't you think Joan should be told?"

"She knows, too!" Mavis said, close to tears. "She's forgiven him. Don't you see she loves him?"

Tom stared, mouth agape. A quiet rage overcoming him

"Why does tha' always stick up for him?" he shouted.

"Stick up for him? I hate his guts! I hate him more than you do! I'm not sticking up for him. I'm sticking up for Joan and you should be, too. I'm thinking of her!"

Having said this, his wife sank her head onto the table and sobbed. Tom slowly rose from his chair, kissed her greying hair and said "Goodnight, my love," before going to bed.

"Tomorrow…" Tom thought, "…tomorrow, I will sort this out once and for all… That excuse for a man 'as caused too much damage to my family. Tomorrow it all ends!"

*****

The following day was a Saturday, and Tom had a lie in before joining his wife for a cooked breakfast. She seemed more relaxed, as it appeared that Tom had accepted the situation that existed between Joan and Winston. The weather was atrocious. The snow that had been falling all night had not stopped and a light wind had sent the temperatures plummeting. After a wash and shave Tom shrugged into his heavy, woollen overcoat.

"You are not going out in this?" questioned Mavis.

"Just popping out for some pipe 'baccy', love, won't be long," he said, giving her a peck on the cheek. He was heading for Joan's flat in Lumpton to confront Winston. He wasn't sure what he was going to do, but he knew it wouldn't be a wasted journey.

On the outskirts of Tollthorpe, where the road led to Lumpton, there was a pub called The Fox and Hounds. Tom decided to call for a quick drink before trudging the three miles through the snow to Joan's flat. The bar was almost empty, but he was greeted by the barman.

"Hey up, Tommy. We don't often see you in here."
"Just a swift one, Paul, I've a few things to do. A whisky please."
"You have just missed him," said Paul.
"Just missed who?" frowned Tom.
"That lad of Joan's - left about twenty minutes ago."
"Wasn't looking for him, Paul," lied Tom, noting the clock showed 1pm.
"Yeah, he tried cadging his taxi fare home, but we weren't having it. Always scrounging. Oops! Sorry, Tommy, wasn't thinking!"
"Don't worry, Paul. There is nothing you can say about that waster that will upset me!" snorted Tom, lifting the glass to his lips.

Paul laughed and said, "He set off walking. He only had a thin coat on...he'll be freezing his bollocks off!"

The road to Lumpton was mostly straight with just a few bends, hedged fields at either side and no pavements. Visibility was very bad and he made sure he walked facing any oncoming traffic, though that was unlikely in these conditions.

Half an hour into his walk and he was beginning to falter, snow driving into his face. He had just taken a bend in the road when he stopped; he was sure that he had heard something. The wind dropped and there it was again. Was that a faint call for help coming from the ditch on the other side of the road? Hurrying over he squinted down into the ditch and saw the huddled form of Robert Winston.

"Who is it?" cried Winston.
"Oh, thank God, thank God, it's thee, Mr Fletcher. Some bastard hit me with a car and drove off! I think I've broken both me legs! It's me, Robert. I've been here ages. I'm freezing to death! You've got to get help! Get an ambulance! Please, Tom, be quick! It's me, Robert!"
Tom looked straight into the waster's eyes and smiled. Winston looked back in horror.
"No, no, it's me, Robert! Get help!"
Tom turned and slowly walked back towards Tollthorpe. The waster's pleas growing fainter and fainter as the snow closed in.

Robert Winston's frozen body was found later that day by a man walking his dog. Winston had been right about the broken legs, but it was the cold that killed him.

The hit-and-run driver was never found.

*****

It had stopped falling, but snow lay heavy on the ground as the funeral cortege ghosted up to the Fletcher's front door. Tom helped his wife into a waiting car and they followed the hearse as it made its way slowly up to the small village cemetery.

Standing by the open grave with the other mourners, Tom held Mavis's arm as they watched the coffin being lowered slowly into the cold earth.

The brass plate on the coffin lid bore the name:

JOAN WINSTON

Three days after the wasters' body had been found, Joan was found dead on her bed by an anxious neighbour. Beside her, an empty bottle that had once contained sleeping tablets.

As no note was found the police recorded the death, perhaps through kindness, as an open verdict. But everyone knew that it was suicide.

"I'm so sorry, love. I'm so, so sorry…" Tom told Mavis. "It's not your fault, Tom. You didn't kill her!"

"Oh, but I did, love. Oh, but I did!" he sobbed.

Then, head bowed, Tommy Fletcher walked slowly through the snow, towards the cemetery gates.

The Engine Shed

High heels clicking on the dance room floor
to the rock and roll music that opened youth's door.
The girls: they swirl, pivot, jive,
to the songs and the music that kept dreams alive.
The tempo it rises, and the years have fled,
on Saturday night at the Engine Shed.

Don, he wrote, of the music dying,
with Buddy, and others, in a plane crash lying.
But their music lives on and we smile at the times,
when barefooted, in bedrooms had door handle jives.
The lights now are flashing, floor speckled in red,
on Saturday night at the Engine Shed.

Pretty frocks swirling, waist belt high,
'Teds' in their drapes and boot lace tie.
The ghosts of old rock stars look down and smile;
these people are ours, at least for a while.
Mavis is to the dance floor led,
on Saturday night at the Engine Shed.

The clock is calling; time for one last dance,
As the platters lament a lost romance.
Couples sway to the rhythm and remember past times
of hurried back door kisses to church clock chimes.
The music dies and our memories shred
on Saturday night at the Engine Shed.

Footnote

The Engine Shed is a Working Men's Club in the village of Wetherby in North Yorkshire, not far from where I am presently living in Knaresborough.

Once a month, they have a fifties nostalgia night. This is when all the old 'Teddy Boys' along with their girls, dress up in their fifties rock and roll regalia and dance the night away.

I can recall seeing 'Teds' on the streets as a schoolboy, and they seemed to give off an air of menace, which I am now sure was self-cultivated and there was little or no harm in them. I was astonished how well they danced and how much I liked their music, particularly the ballads of that period. I envied them their night in the past and was happy for them.

Unable to dance myself, I wrote this poem, which started its life on the back of a beer mat.

Ghost Catcher

Martin Hopkins sighed heavily as he eased himself into his favourite armchair; a glass of Famous Grouse topped up with American Dry in his hand. It was one of the few comforts in his life along with his music and books, the books being mainly biographies. Although he owned a television, he hated the gruel that was force fed to viewers on a daily basis: cheap reality shows, featuring factory made celebrities with a shelf life of fifteen minutes; repeats after repeats; endless cooking shows. He only watched documentaries, the News and, very occasionally, a film. He resented bitterly having to pay for a television licence when, for him, it was such poor value. The scary thing were the kids who were brought up on this bilge water not knowing any better.

He lived in a comfortable semi-detached bungalow in Northolt, in the London Borough of Ealing, a fifteen minute train ride from his work place in White City. Hopkins had worked for May and Hughes Insurance Brokers for twenty eight years as a Risk Assessment Officer, slowly rising to become head of his department. He was not at all ambitious. Therefore, the senior management did not see him as a threat. He was forty eight years old, and both management and he knew that he would be holding his present position until death, retirement or redundancy forced him out. He could not have cared less.

Hopkin's colleagues and neighbours would have described him as a mild, quietly spoken man, always smartly dressed in a Marks and Spencer's kind of way, always wore a tie and highly polished brogues.

A *ping!* announced that his microwave meal was ready and he reproached himself for being lazy. The truth was, that since his wife, May, had died of cancer ten years ago, he couldn't be bothered peeling potatoes. Having said that, he kept the bungalow spotless. Everything had its place; not a cushion out of line. He often wondered if he had some form of obsessive compulsive disorder.

In short, Martin Hopkins was a nice man who led a very boring and uneventful life, and he would not have had it any other way. What Martin Hopkins didn't know, was that in just a few short days his life would change in a way that he would never have dreamed possible, nor would anyone else for that matter.

*****

After his morning shower, he inspected himself in the bedroom's full length mirror. Though never a vain man, he prided himself on his appearance. Staring back at him, he saw a middle aged man, short in stature, carrying a bit of a paunch, clean shaven with receding salt and pepper hair. His redeeming feature was his pale blue eyes of which he was secretly proud. Someone had once commented that he looked a bit like the actor, Antony Hopkins, and this had pleased him. Perhaps he was a little vain after all.

After checking that the bungalow was secure three times, he made his way to the Central Line train station. The usual Thursday morning crowd dotted the platform, ready for their daily, short commute into London. He nodded to a few of the familiar faces. He had been seeing these same faces for years, yet he could not recall having spoken to any of them.

Entering the offices of May and Hughes, just off Wood Lane, he "Morning-ed!" the receptionist, before taking the lift to his third floor office. The time was exactly 9am.

He had twenty staff under his supervision, their desks lined up in four rows of five. His particular desk was encased in a glass partition overlooking the office floor. Most of the staff were positioned around the ancient coffee machine when they should have been at their stations working, yet his entrance hardly caused a stir. He knew that his staff had no respect for him and took advantage of his mild-mannered nature. But they were always polite to him and he felt that many of them liked him - in a condescending sort of way.

Closing the glass door to his office, he lined his pens neatly on his desk, and began work on the large pile of paperwork before him. He was frequently interrupted by many of the younger staff, knocking on his door, requesting him to have a look at a certain case file that they were having trouble with. Hopkins knew that they could resolve these matters with a bit of effort - they were just too lazy to do so. They were essentially palming their workload onto him, but he just smiled and pointed to his desk.

Most of his staff went to the pub at lunchtime, with the exception of Wendy Fettle. Both Wendy and he would purchase sandwiches from a company that toured the offices selling food and snacks from a basket.

Wendy was a mousey looking woman in her fifties with a preference for hand-knitted, brightly coloured cardigans. She had been with the company almost as long as Hopkins. He was never quite sure if she fancied him or just felt sorry for him; whatever the case, she was a good worker, and he wished he had more Wendy Fettles on his staff.

Hopkins entered his bungalow through a pyramid of junk mail. Placing the few groceries he had bought at the corner shop on the kitchen counter, he shrugged off his old trench coat. This coat was one of the few things he possessed that was shoddy, but he liked it, and felt that it gave him a rakish air. Throwing a chicken tikka masala with pilau rice into the microwave, he selected a jazz album and placed it onto the turntable of his old radiogram.

He owned a vast collection of jazz records, all neatly labelled and stored on shelves. All the greats were there: John Coltrane; Thelonious Monk; Duke Ellington; Ella Fitzgerald; Charlie Parker; Louis Armstrong; and, one of his favourites, Chet Baker. He disliked the experimental jazz of Miles Davis and was not keen on Billie Holiday.

These albums were supplemented with a smaller collection from artists such as, Johnny Mathis and Nat King Cole. His wife had preferred country and western which he hated with a vengeance. One of the first things he did after her funeral was to bin all of her albums, although he later felt guilty about it.

Ella Fitzgerald had won the toss and she was half way through *Blue Moon* when the microwave *pinged!*

Tomorrow was Friday, the one day in the week that he met up with his only friend, Sol Cohen, after work. Unbeknownst to Hopkins, tomorrow's meeting would never take place.

Hopkins had first met Sol Cohen one Friday night about three years ago. He had been working late and, hurrying to catch his train, he'd been caught in a thunder storm of biblical proportions. Passing The Turks Head pub, he decided to seek refuge there. He had passed this small pub hundreds of times on his way home from work, but had never before been inside.

Whisky secured, he found a vacant table and, surveying his surroundings, he found them pleasing; old fashioned, a lot of brass, an open fire, and above all, no television or piped music. His observations were interrupted when a voice from a neighbouring table enquired, "Oh! You like Chet Baker then?"

"Pardon?" He replied, turning to face a small, dapper looking man, in what looked to be a very expensive, three piece suit.

"Chet Baker," explained the man, pointing to the album Hopkins had purchased earlier. "You like Chet Baker?"

"Oh! Yes!" Nodded Hopkins, recovering. "Only discovered him quite recently."

"Sol Cohen," said the man, introducing himself and offering a hand.

"Martin Hopkins," he replied, taking his hand.

During the conversation that followed, they discovered that they had similar interests. Mainly jazz and chess, and they agreed to meet in The Turks Head the following Friday. Then, as their friendship developed, it became a weekly routine.

As his name suggests, Sol Cohen was Jewish. Hopkins always thought that Sol resembled the character Poirot from the television series, as portrayed by David Suchet, but without the big belly and moustache.

As if by some unspoken agreement, neither of the men said very much about their personal lives. This seemed to suit the both of them, so, their conversations were of a general nature. They would meet around 6pm in the pub, enjoy a meal together (the pub served surprisingly good food), then retire to a backroom with their drinks and a chess set that they kept behind the bar. They were equally matched at chess. Perhaps Sol had the edge on him, but they enjoyed their chess games and each other's company. Neither were big drinkers; Sol liked a few gin and tonics, and he, of course, his whisky. Around 10pm, Hopkins would bid his farewells, then walk the short distance to a taxi rank around the corner.

Wendy Fettle noticed that Hopkins carried a different demeanour about him on a Friday; he smiled more and kept looking at the clock. She wondered if he had a weekly meeting with a woman…perhaps a prostitute.

"Tony…" nodded Hopkins to the barman, "Whisky, please. No, Sol?" The clock showed 6.20pm. "No, Martin, but he left you this," replied Tony, handing him an envelope. The note inside read, "Dear Martin, sorry I will not be able to make it tonight due to a small family crisis. I may be able to get in for around 9pm, but I cannot guarantee it. So do not feel obliged to wait for me. If I don't see you tonight, I will see you next Friday. Sol."

"Everything OK?" enquired the barman, nodding towards the note.

"Oh! Yes fine. Said he may be in later." He answered frowning. "When did Sol leave this? Earlier today?"

"No," explained Tony, "Last night around seven-ish. Quick drink and he was off. Don't you guys exchange phone numbers?"

"No, we should really. Will do next time I see him," he said, reaching for the menu.

"Funny, the police were asking about him last night," mused Tony. "Hope he is alright!"

He gave it until 9.30pm, waved his goodbye to the barman, and left for the taxi rank. About two hundred yards down from the taxi rank was a small park with a scattering of shrubs and benches. It was a run-down area, but popular with office workers who were able eat their lunch there when the weather permitted. At night it was the haunt of druggies.

Just as he was passing the park, a strange sensation overcame him; things seemed to slip sideways, like frames on a film roll overlapping. The air appeared to thicken and waver. He rested against a wall to recover. Looking up, he saw the unmistakable form of Sol running across the grass. In pursuit, was a man waving something in his hand.

Both figures appeared to be running in slow motion. "Sol! Sol!" he shouted and set off after them. To his surprise, he too seemed to be running in slow motion. "Sol! Sol!" he shouted again, "It's me, Martin!" He felt like he was running through treacle. The man caught up with Sol and pushed him to the ground. Then, to Hopkins' horror, he saw something flashing in the street lights and realised that Sol was being stabbed. Sol's assailant appeared to be shouting something, but no sound was coming from him. Hopkins threw himself beside his friend who was screaming a silent scream. His attacker struck a final blow, before searching Sol's limp, blood-soaked body, and removing his wallet and watch. Throughout the entire period, neither Sol, nor the man, appeared to have registered Hopkins' presence. His screams for help seemed to have gone unheard by everyone, including the knifeman, who was now standing and looking about him. Hopkins, now fearing for his own life, was surprised when the man mimed a chuckle, threw the knife into a bush, and ran from the park.

Hopkins had never owned a mobile phone. He ran, screaming for help, to the pub. The air around him had shifted again and his movements appeared normal. The police found him shaking and crying in the corner of The Turks Head, with the barman trying to coax a whisky down him. After a search, no body was found and the ambulance was sent away. The police, shaking their heads, were about to drive him home, when he mentioned Sol Cohen's name, and everything changed.

Hopkins was asked if wanted hospital treatment before being driven the eight miles to New Scotland Yard on the Victoria embankment.

"Mr Hopkins, please take a seat. Can I get you anything?" This was from an attractive woman in her early forties. "My name is Detective Chief Inspector Burton and this is Detective Sergeant Betts," she said, indicating a ginger haired man, who looked like he should still be at school. "We are part of the Serious Crime Squad. We need to ask you a few questions regarding Mr Cohen."
"That's what I have been trying to tell everyone. I witnessed his murder tonight. What's wrong with everybody?"

"OK, OK, calm down! First, we need to take your particulars. Then, I want you to start from the very beginning and tell me everything you know about Sol Cohen. Do you mind if we record this?"

Nearly an hour later, Hopkins had explained to DCI Burton about his weekly meetings with Sol and what had happened that night.

"Do you have the note Mr Cohen left for you?" Burton was furious that, on being questioned earlier, the barman at The Turks Head had not mentioned the note.

"Yes, of course!" he said, handing it over.

"We will have to keep this," Burton said, sliding it into a drawer.

"Where is Sol? He can't have disappeared. He must have crawled off somewhere. You should be out there looking for him. Maybe he is still alive?" shouted Hopkins.

"I am afraid Mr Cohen is dead, Mr Hopkins. We have him in the morgue. Now, let's go back to what you saw tonight. Describe the man you say killed your friend."

"About five foot ten; not tall. Very heavily built. Wearing a light tan, cheap-looking, leather jacket. Those pants with lots of pockets…?"

"Cargo pants?" offered Burton.

"Yes, yes, cargo pants, and trainers. I don't think he was wearing gloves."

"Hair colour?" asked Burton.

"Don't know. He had one of those woolly hats on. Are they called 'beanies'? He was white but looked foreign."

"Mr Hopkins, in all my years on the Force, I have never had such a precise description of someone given to me, bearing in mind it was dark and you were under stress."

"It's my job to note detail. I am a Risk Assessment Officer and I was sat right next to the bloody man for Christ's sake!" exploded Hopkins.

"Tell me…" Burton asked, "…why didn't the man attack you? And why didn't you try to save your friend?"

"I told you, he didn't seem to see me, and I did try to save Sol!"

"How did you try to save Sol?"

"I tried to pull the man off him!"

"And…?" from Burton.

Silence followed.

"Mr Hopkins…and? Mr Hopkins, you need to answer my question. What happened when you tried to pull the man off?"

"My hands went right through his body, like he was a ghost." He lowered his head as Burton and Betts looked at each other in amazement. "You think I killed him, don't you?" he shouted, standing up.

"No, I don't think you killed him, Mr Hopkins, and sit down. Indeed, I know for a fact that you didn't kill him, at least, not tonight. What would you say, Mr Hopkins, if I was to tell you that your friend was stabbed to death between 7pm and 8pm last night, not tonight, in exactly the same spot you indicated to police officers this evening? We know this because officers questioned the bar staff in The

Turks Head and they confirmed that Mr Cohen left the pub at 7pm and CCTV footage confirms this. Then, an hour later at 8pm, a man walking his dog found the body. So you see, we have a small window here, one hour, which makes our job a lot easier. So, all you have to do, Mr Hopkins, is satisfy us as to your whereabouts between 7pm and 8pm last night." Hopkins obliged. "We will be checking that out. You can go now. It's late. I will arrange for a car to take you home."

Burton looked down from her office window as Hopkins got into the Police car. "Weird, bloody weird!" she muttered. Then, turning suddenly, she said, "Sergeant, take a few men down to the spot where Cohen was murdered and check those bushes again. You are looking for a knife. Didn't Hopkins say the man threw the knife into a bush?"

"Now ma'am?"
"Yes, bloody now!" barked Burton.
"But we searched the area thoroughly yesterday!" protested Betts.
"Then search it again! You have torches don't you? Just get on with it!"

Detective Chief Inspector Burton had just arrived home when her mobile sounded. "It's Betts. We think we may have found the knife that was used to kill Cohen."

*****

"Find anything on Hopkins, Jenny?"

Monday morning and the office was buzzing after the discovery of the knife. WPC Jenny Houston looked up from her computer.

"Nothing ma'am. Clean as a whistle. No history. Wife died ten years ago. Daughter, June, teaches in Manchester; married name Preston. Never owned a car. No driving license. Never owned a passport. Worked for May and Hughes for twenty eight years. Is this guy alive?"

"What about his alibi for Thursday?" prompted Burton.

"Left his office at 6.32pm. The security guard that comes on at 6pm booked him out. It is also on CCTV. Platform camera shows him catching the train from White City to Northolt at 7.02pm. Caught on camera arriving at Northolt at 7.20pm. Finally, CCTV footage of him on Northolt High Street carrying shopping at 7.53pm. No way could he have been at the murder scene."

"Thanks, Jenny. Sergeant, what news on the knife?"
"Forensic results back at midday, ma'am."
"You wanted to see me, sir?" Chief Superintendent, John Savage, looked up from his desk.
"Yes, Jill. I believe congratulations are in order!" Three weeks had passed since Cohens' body had been found.
"Three weeks from the murder and a man charged. Must be some kind of record." John Savage was a gruff Yorkshire man with very bushy eye brows. He did not suffer fools gladly.

"I couldn't have done it so quickly, if at all, without Hopkins' help," admitted Burton.

"Ah, yes, the psychic chappie!"

"I don't know what he is, sir, but every single bit of information he gave us was spot on. It was like having an eyewitness at the scene. We would not have had the knife if not for him - we missed it on the first search. The blood on the knife matched Cohen's and the fingerprints on the knife we had on file: a Lithuanian named Sergi Savos. We even found the clothing that Hopkins described with blood stains on them. So hardly a great bit of detective work on my part, sir. Hopkins handed him to us on a plate."

"Good work, anyway. How's the 'homeless man in the warehouse' investigation going? ID'd the body yet?" asked Savage, pausing to sip his coffee.

"Hit a brick wall with that one, sir. We are getting nowhere," sighed Burton. "So, what's your next move, Jill?"

"Well, sir, I was thinking of asking Martin Hopkins for help…"

The Superintendents' bushy eyebrows nearly shot off the top of his head!

*****

Hopkins saw the unmarked police car pull up and DCI Burton get out from behind the steering wheel. Pulling her long, blue, woollen scarf up against the cold, she headed towards his door. Dropping the curtain, he muttered, "What now?" before going to open the door. "Sorry to bother you on your day off," offered Burton, "Don't worry, it's not an official visit as such. May I come in?"

He returned with a tray of tea and biscuits to find her admiring the Grandfather Clock which was standing in the hall. "What a beautiful clock. I have always wanted one. Walnut case, isn't it?"

"Maple, actually. What is the purpose of your visit, Inspector?" he said, pouring the tea.

"Well, first, I would like to apologise for the treatment you received at the station. I was a bit hard on you."

"Understandable under the circumstances. You take sugar?"

"No thanks, just milk. You are aware we have charged a man with Mr Cohen's murder?"

Handing her a cup of tea, he nodded. "Yes, I read about it in the papers."

"From what we can gather, Mr Cohens' mother had been taken ill and the nursing home where she resides had moved her into hospital. He was on his way to visit her when he was murdered. We believe he had planned another visit for the following night. That is why he left you the note."

"This man charged with his murder…" began Hopkins.

"Sergi Savos; a druggie from Lithuania. We believe he had seen Sol leave the pub, noted how well dressed he was, and the expensive watch, and decided to mug him - a mugging that ended in murder!" interrupted Burton. "Are you aware that your friend was a very wealthy man? He owned a precious stone business in Hatton Gardens and a small jewellery shop. Very well respected. Gave a lot to charity."

"No, I wasn't aware of that, but it doesn't surprise me. Did he have any family?" he asked, offering a biscuit.

"Only his mother. His wife died two years ago in a car crash. Mr Hopkins, the main reason I am here today is to speak to you about what you saw that Friday night. Have you ever experienced anything like that before?"

"No, never. It troubled me that the police had been asking about Sol the night before. I was thinking about him on the way to the taxi rank, then I became nauseous and time seemed to slip sideways." He stopped. "I am not making much sense, am I?"

"All I know is that the information you gave to us was accurate in every detail, and I mean *every* detail. Had it not been for you, we would not have found the knife. There were a few red faces on my team the following morning, I can tell you!" she said, nibbling a biscuit.

"Two things I don't get," he said, scratching his head, "Surely the bar staff would have been aware of the murder by Friday night when I was in? Also, why am I not being summoned to give evidence in court?"

"To answer your first question, they would have been aware that something had happened. People would have seen the police activity and police tape Thursday night. The fact that it was a murder scene would not have gone to the Press until the weekend. To answer your second question, everything you told us about Sol's murder could never be used in court. Try explaining to a jury that you witnessed a murder the day after it was committed, but that doesn't mean the information you gave to us was any the less valuable. It was like having an eyewitness account. Only we could not present that witness in court. Any more tea? That brings me to the real reason for my visit, Mr Hopkins… May I call you Martin?"

*****

Detective Sergeant Betts pulled to a halt on the rugged forecourt of the abandoned warehouse on the South Bank. DCI Burton stepped out of the car straight into a puddle. "Thank you, sergeant!" she said. "Sorry, ma'am!" replied Betts, with just the hint of a smirk on his face. Burton did not like Betts and had been trying to offload him for months. Betts was academically blessed with a cartload of qualifications, but he was a lazy copper who found everything too much trouble. He was next to useless on the street and was obviously destined for a desk job, which was where he belonged and was what he probably wanted. "Please come with me, Martin," she urged Hopkins. She led him into the warehouse that stank of shit and piss. Taking him to a small room at the back, which was probably once an office, she asked him to concentrate and tell her what he saw, if anything. She had told him nothing about the case that involved the horrific murder of a homeless man. His body had been discovered two days ago. But the autopsy report showed that he had died two days prior to his body being found. He had been beaten to death, probably with a baseball bat, before being doused with petrol and set on fire.

After extensive inquiries, all Burton could come up with was that he was homeless, in his sixties, Scottish, an alcoholic, and that his name was probably Ted. This information was gleaned from various homeless people on being given a description of him. The top half of his body was untouched by the fire. Despite this, no dental or fingerprint match was found, so she was unable to find a surname. Even a nationwide newspaper appeal had drawn a blank. There appeared to be no motive for his death. She was hoping Martin would be able to help.

"You getting anything, Martin?"

"No, sorry, nothing much." The air around him had rippled a little and in the weak, winters light that came in through the glassless windows, he saw the vague outline of a bearded man. It was very faint and the image kept fading in and out. He explained what he had seen to Burton, which was not much. Burton was unable to hide her disappointment, "Well, thanks for trying, Martin. I appreciate it!"

"Oh! Before I forget…" she handed him a white envelope.

"What's this?" He enquired.

"Your fee. I hope you find it adequate."

"But I have not done anything!" protested Hopkins.

"You gave us your time and effort, and you should be paid for that," said Burton. On the way back to the car, Burton stopped to talk to PC Alan Crosby. He was with the dog unit. "Hello, Alan. Find anything?" What Alan told her made her pause for thought. I wonder, I just wonder, she pondered…

Burton had known PC Alan Crosby for years. He was close to retirement and he and his present dog, a collie named

Shep, planned to retire together. Burton had a soft spot for the old guy. Alan had been sent for in the vague hope that he and Shep could find the murder weapon. But Alan had explained to her that there was little hope of that, as the murder scene had gone cold. "You see, ma'am, you have got to get the dogs in as early as possible. Any scents fade after time, particularly outdoors with the rain and wind. The longer you leave it, the less chance the dog has. I believe the poor sod has been dead for four days now." Burton patted Shep on the head, wished them both a happy retirement, and carried her thoughts to the waiting car.

The following morning saw Burton back in Chief Superintendent Savage's office. "So, you drew a blank, Jill?"

"Well, yes," admitted Burton, "But I think I know why!" She then went on to repeat the conversation she had with the dog handler.

"Your point being…?" asked Savage, reaching for a cigarette, before remembering the no smoking rule.

"Don't you see? What if it's the same with Hopkins? Maybe we have to get him to the murder scene earlier?! Maybe the energies, or whatever they are, fade in time, like the scent that the dogs try to pick up. Hopkins did see faint images, but this was four days after the vagrant was murdered. It's got to be worth another try! I will do it in my own time and pay his fee out of my own pocket. If I am unsuccessful, I promise the matter will end there. I will never mention Hopkins' name again. But just think, if he provides the goods, it will give any investigation a jump start. Not to mention the thousands of pounds saved in man hours!"

"So, what are you suggesting?" sighed Savage.

"That recent murder in Shepherd's Bush; the bedsit one that DCI Morris is running. Why don't I try Hopkins on that one? We know the murder is only a day old. Just one more time…?" pleaded Burton.

Savage was deep in thought for what seemed like an age, before saying, "Right, I will tell you what I will do, if, and I mean, *if*, DCI Morris agrees to it, I will allow it this one time. Then, I want you back on the warehouse case. No arguments! Got it?"

"Yes, thank you, sir!"

"I am buggered if I know why I indulge you, Jill."

"That would be because I am sexy with a cute, little dimple on my chin!" smiled Burton.

"Out!" barked Savage, chuckling to himself as the door closed behind her.

*****

Burton was treating Hopkins to a pub lunch. Explaining her theory, she asked him to give it another try. Hopkins was reluctant but eventually agreed to it. As they were leaving, Burton commented on the expensive looking, gold watch that he wore on his wrist. "Nice watch, Martin."

"Yes," he said, "A present from my daughter on my fortieth birthday." Slipping it off, he showed her the inscription on the back. It read:

To Dad, on your 40th Birthday. Love June x

Burton and Hopkins met DCI Morris outside the bedsit of the raped and murdered girl. A black girl, twenty eight years old, named Susan Swain.

"A waste of bloody time, if you ask me," Morris muttered, "But get on with it!"

"Thanks, Ken!" she said, pinching his cheek.

As before, Burton had not told Hopkins any details about the case. He only knew what he had read in the papers. The air around Hopkins thickened and stirred, time seemed to slip sideways. He described the scene in great detail, then vomited in the corner. The girl had been brutally raped then strangled with a pair of tights. He described the man as Asian, wearing a pair of overalls with 'British Gas' written on them. Before leaving, the man removed a gold charm bracelet from the girls' wrist. Hopkins had not seen a charm bracelet for years. They were popular in the sixties, but were considered old fashioned now. Burton knew that the mother of the dead girl had reported the bracelet missing. Once belonging to the mother, she had passed it on to her daughter.

It was on hearing of the bracelet that Burton knew for sure that Hopkins was genuine and that he possessed a strange gift. The missing bracelet had purposely been held back from the Press. There was no way Hopkins could have known about it beforehand. Thanking Hopkins, she ran him home, then returned to the office to write out her report. Now she and Hopkins were finished with the case, it was down to DCI Ken Morris to solve the murder, which he did three months later. An Asian man working for British Gas was charged and convicted of the murder. The charm bracelet was found in his possession. DCI Ken Morris was delighted because, of course, he got all the credit. Hopkins' input was not mentioned in his report. In fact, he had been told specifically that no mention of Hopkins was to be made, either verbally or in writing.

*****

On their way to where a body had been found by the side of the A20 leading to Kent, Hopkins had informed Burton that this was to be the last one. "I know you pay me well," he said, "But it's too much with my work load at May and Hughes as well."

"I understand, Martin," she nodded. "Let's just see what we can get from this one."

She rolled the car to a standstill, next to a marker that had been placed near to where the body had been found earlier that morning. Standing on the grass verge, Hopkins gazed down over the flattened grass. As usual, he had been given no details about the case.

"Young male, seventeen…eighteen years old. White with what could be gang tattoos…" he described the tattoos, "Grey bomber jacket, torn jeans. Gunshot wounds to the head." All this of course Burton knew.

"Can you see who killed him, Martin?"

"No, he wasn't killed here."

"What! What did you say?"

"He wasn't killed here, Jill. His body was dumped here last night."

"How do you know it was last night?" she said, astounded.

"Because the area in which he is lying in, or was lying in, is shrouded in darkness, even though it is daylight now."

"Christ!" exclaimed Burton. "Do you know who dumped him here and at what time?"

Hopkins rubbed his chin. "Two young lads driving a red Ford Fiesta with a damaged, nearside wing. They pulled his body from the boot and threw it onto the verge." He then went on to give a description of the two youths and the registration of the car. "Sorry, Jill, I have no way of knowing what time this took place. Oh! Just a moment, he is wearing a watch!"

To Burton's disbelief, Hopkins got down on his hands and knees and, to her, he seemed to be looking at nothing but a patch of flattened grass. "His watch shows 11.42..." grinned Hopkins, "I am assuming that is pm?"

"They are not going to believe this back at the station," said Burton, as she got back into her car.

*****

Detective Inspector Mark Turner, who was investigating the murder, could not believe his luck. He read Burton's report again, even the bloody car registration, and shook his head in wonder.

The office fell silent as Burton swept in. All eyes were upon her. "Jesus, Jill. What have you done?" whispered PC Jenny Houston. "They are all in there!"

"Who's all in where?" said Burton.

"The bloody lot. All the top brass. Commander Blake, the Deputy Assistant Commissioner and the Assistant Commissioner. Everyone except The Queen Mother. All in the Superintendent's office waiting for you!" Jenny's eyes were like saucers.

Right on cue, John Savage opened his office door and beckoned Burton in. For the next hour, Burton was subjected to a barrage of questions concerning Hopkins - the murder scenes he had attended, the outcome of his visits. Even though she could see they had all of Hopkins' files before them, the questions kept coming. "OK, Inspector," Superintendent Savage said kindly, "We will call you when we need you."

They needed her half an hour later. She came back out of the office smiling, going straight up to Detective Sergeant Mel Betts, who had taken great delight in the thought that she may be in trouble, and said, "Got a promotion, cocksucker?" This was not true, but she had got rid of Betts.

*****

"Martin, it's Jill. Can we meet? I have a proposition for you. Tonight? Great. Eight o'clock, OK? Fine, see you then." She replaced the receiver. She had not seen Hopkins since the A20 incident three weeks before.

"Hello, Jill. I have not changed my mind you know…!" he said, opening the door.

"All I want you to do is hear me out, Martin, without interruption," she replied, handing him a bottle of Laphroaig, ten year old, single malt whisky.

"What's this?" he asked, taking the bottle and studying the label.

"A present from me," she smiled. "Don't worry; it's not a bribe!"

"Thank you, Jill. That's a very expensive whisky!"

"You are welcome," she said, sitting down.

"OK, here is the proposition: This is from the Deputy Assistant Commissioner of the Met, no less. The Met would like to employ you full time. Your salary will be a twenty percent increase on what you are presently receiving at May and Hughes. The Met would be payrolling you as a Police Adviser: a title that covers a multitude of sins. You would not have to report to the office in the morning, you simply have to wait until you are contacted. It may be weeks or even months before we contact you, but your salary will still be secured. You will be working inclusively with me. You may be asked to travel with me to aid police forces nationwide. As you know, we only have a three day window on this, then the murder scene begins to fade."

"What you mean…" he interrupted.

"Let me finish, Martin. If you have to travel outside the Met, all of your expenses will be covered; that is to say food and accommodation. In return, the Met expects you to be available day and night, at any time. You must never speak to anyone about what you do - this is mainly for security reasons. The less people know about your talent, the better. This is for your own safety! Any chance of a cup of tea?"

"Yes, of course. What about my job at May and Hughes?"

"You will have to resign, of course. Your initial contract will be for six months. After that, if the Met is happy with you, and you are happy with the Met, your contract will be extended."

"So, I could be out of work in six months?" he said, pouring the tea.

"Technically, yes, if either party decide to call it a day. But I have that covered and you owe me a drink for this. The Deputy Assistant Commissioner knows the co-owner of May and Hughes, Sir Colin May. I believe they attend the same Masonic Lodge. The Deputy Commissioner has spoken to Sir May and he assures me that, should there be a parting of ways, you will be reinstated at May and Hughes. It may not be in your last post, but the salary will remain the same as when you left. Make that a large drink you owe me!"

"I don't know what to say!" said Hopkins, pouring himself a large whisky.

"Well," replied Burton, "Start by giving me that large drink now and get yourself a bloody mobile phone. Christ, Martin, it's 2014!"

*****

Martin Hopkins was to go on to work for the Met for five years. Initially, he was greeted with scorn and ridicule by the Serious Crime Squad detectives, but it did not take them long to realise that they could benefit greatly from his psychic visions; not only that, they got all the credit!

During his time with the Met, the conviction rate for homicide rose from 66.67% to 94.2%. Of course, Hopkins did not solve the crimes himself, that was down to detective work. But there is no doubt that his skills played a major role in the Mets' success.

Over the years, with Burtons help, he managed to hone his technique. She fitted him up with a throat mic and a recorder so that he could record what was happening as he was seeing it. She even encouraged him to take lip reading lessons. This was because one of the oddities of his visions was, that although he could see people's mouths move, no sound came out. It was like watching a silent movie.

During his first year at the Met, he acquired a nickname. A Senior Officer had asked him what he experienced during a vision. "Well, sir," he explained, "It's a bit like trying to catch ghosts." Henceforth, he was to become known as 'The Ghost Catcher'…and a legend was born.

*****

It was at the end of 2019 when Hopkins told Burton that he wanted to go back to his old job. "It's getting to me, Jill. You only see the aftermath of a killing which is bad enough. But I see the actual killing! The worst part is that I am getting blasé about it!" Burton hugged him and said that she was just surprised he had lasted so long. They had worked together for five years and had become very close; not in a romantic way, but close nevertheless. Hopkins planned to work at May and Hughes for another seven years. Then, on reaching sixty, taking early retirement. He would never reach retirement age.

"Jill? It's Martin. Can you meet me for a drink tonight?"

"Sure, Martin. The Bulls Head at eight?"

"That's fine."

"Everything OK, Martin? You sound a bit odd?"

"I have a bit of unsettling news. I will tell you about it when I see you."

On Hopkins leaving the Met a year ago, Burton had gone back to her previous role as Detective Chief Inspector in the Serious Crime Squad. She did not see a lot of Hopkins; they probably met up once or twice a month for a drink or a meal. He even attempted to teach her how to play chess, but she just did not have the patience for it.

Once they had settled down with their drinks, Burton said, "OK, what's the problem?"

"Well, I would like to report a murder!" said Hopkins, looking her right in the eye.

"Whose murder, Martin?"

"Mine, Jill! Mine!"

Burton let out a guffaw of laughter. "My, you have been overworked!"

Hopkins just looked at her. "Martin, the fact that you are talking to me means that you have not been murdered."

"Not yet, but I will be very shortly," he said quietly.

"How do you know?" she demanded.

"I have seen it! Three youths will break into my bungalow, stab and rob me… I don't know when, but soon. I have put my affairs in order. I thought that you might want a description of the youths to aid your inquiries."

"People can't see into the future, Martin!" she said, exasperated.

"People can't usually witness a murder days after it happened. But I can!" His hand reached out for hers. "Jill, it's important to remember that the one with red hair stabbed me and took my watch just seconds before I died."

*****

It was four days later. Hopkins was sipping his whisky and listening to Chet Baker singing, *It's Always You*, when the door burst open. He put down his drink and rose to accept his fate…

On hearing the news at the station, Detective Chief Inspector Burton fainted for the first time in her life.

*****

It was a spring morning, two months later, and Jill Burton was placing flowers on Martin Hopkins grave.

"We got them, Martin! We got the bastards! The red haired one, Jackson, tried selling your watch to, believe it or not, Sol Cohen's jewellery shop. Noting the inscription on the watch, it was obvious to the jeweller that eighteen year old Jackson, was not the owner. So, he refused to buy the watch and called the police. So, then we examined the shops CCTV footage of him. I have retrieved your watch and sent it to your daughter. So, Martin, you were 'The Ghost Catcher' to the very end. Thank you for leaving me the beautiful Grandfather Clock. I will always treasure it. I love and miss you, Martin."

On saying that, she kissed her fingers and placed them on top of the headstone. Turning to leave, a gentle breeze lifted her fine, blonde hair, and Martins' voice whispered in her ear, "Love you, too, Jill!"

The Ghost

Home from the trenches: the blood, fear and gore,
my Army boots lying on the bedroom floor.
The cold is relentless as I shiver in bed,
greatcoat hanging on the backdoor peg.

I miss my wife who death snatched away,
just days before I came home to stay.
I see her now in slumber beside me;
her sweet love and kisses forever denied me.

We have a child. My first time of seeing
her cot in the corner; she is all of my being.
The coals in the grate, die out and fall,
shadows advance from the bedroom wall.

Little Mary; for that is her name,
cries out in her sleep and fills me with shame.
I leap from my bed to reach down and hold her,
but stopped when a presence appeared at my shoulder,

for there, in the shadows, my wife stood and stared;
conflicting emotions, her lovely face shared.
Then, to my horror and anguish, she let out a cry:
for, you see, The Ghost was I.

Footnote

I have always been interested in the notion that perhaps some ghosts are unaware that they are dead.

This is not a new idea, and has been portrayed in many films – noticeably, 'Ghost', 'Sixth Sense' and, probably the best of the lot, 'The Others'. The latter of which, very cleverly, had a double plot twist at the end.

My poem, *The Ghost*, started with just the last line, "For, you see, The Ghost was I" rattling around in my head, and I worked down to that line.

I found it hard to write; I did not wish to deceive the reader. When I wrote of the soldier losing his wife, it was true. When he died, he *had* lost his wife; it works both ways.

I was very pleased with the result.

Peter the Death

The BSA Bantam spluttered its way along the narrow country road that led to Brimham Rocks in, what was then, the North Riding of Yorkshire. High hedgerows obscured most of the views and dawdling pheasants were a constant menace.

Lee Penn nursed the little bike around the corners. Its small, 175cc engine growling when he changed down a gear. The autumn sun dappled the road and a slight chill hung in the air. Lee was feeling good. He had bought the bike second-hand, after months of squirrelling away what was left of his wages, after paying his mother board and lodgings. He kept his speed down to 35mph, enjoying the wind in his hair; crash helmets were not yet compulsory.

Approaching a tight corner, he changed down a gear and lent into it. Straightening the bike, he was momentarily blinded by the sun and he lost valuable seconds before seeing the tractor emerging from a gated field. Braking hard, he fishtailed towards the tractor, and for a moment, thought he would be able to squeeze past it. Then, to his dismay, he saw that the tractor was pulling a trailer. Lee had a vague memory of sailing over the trailer and a blinding flash as his head struck something. Then, nothing but darkness.

*****

Lee awoke to the sound of a familiar voice. Slowly, he opened his eyes, and when they focused, he saw his mother sitting beside his bed. On seeing his eyes open, she screamed, "Nurse, nurse, he's opened his eyes!" The noise went through his head like a hacksaw blade. Then he heard the running of feet and a nurse was hovering over him.

"Doctor! Doctor!" she shouted.

Why the Hell is everyone shouting? Another figure joined the nurse.

"Hello, Lee. Can you tell me your name?"

"Lee," he croaked. God he would give anything for a glass of water.

"No, I mean your surname," laughed the doctor, whilst his mother just sobbed. After a series of questions and answers, followed by an examination, the doctor patted him on the shoulder and left. "I need a drink, Mum!" he gasped. His mother brought him a glass of water and he spilt half of it in his eagerness to drink it. "Where am I, mum?"

"Harrogate hospital. Where do you think you are? How do you feel?"

"Got a bit of a headache," Lee replied. His mother looked at him in disbelief.

"A bit of a bloody headache. You have been unconscious for a whole day. You are lucky to be alive! Do you remember what happened?"

Lee thought for a moment, then said, "Yes, the bike. Is it alright?" He thought his Mother was going to strangle him…!

Elsie Penn, aged forty one, was still a good-looking woman and Lee had seen many a male eye cast in her direction. Dad had died three years ago and with Lee being her only child, they had become very close.

The doctor returned and explained to Lee that he had been thrown from his bike and struck his head on the gatepost leading to the field. He had been unconscious for twenty four hours and was probably suffering from concussion. He then went on to say, that having swallowed his tongue, he had stopped breathing for a time, too. Also, he had a gash on his forehead that had required seven stiches. "I'll pop back later. Please don't stay too long, Mrs Penn, he needs to rest."

"Why didn't you wear a crash helmet, Lee?" his mother scolded him.

"I was saving up for one!" protested Lee.

"I would have loaned you the money! Still, it's a bit late now!" his mother sniffed. "I have contacted your work and explained everything, so, don't worry about that."

"Thanks, mum… Mum, who was the tall bloke who came to visit me?" His mother looked at him strangely.

"Nobody's been to visit you. You have been unconscious. You only came out of it ten minutes ago. What did he look like?"

"Well…" explained Lee, "…as I said, tall, dressed in black, handsome, and had a nice smile and kind eyes. In fact, he was the spit of Gregory Peck, the actor."

"Well," said his Mother, "What did he say?"

"Nothing!" replied Lee. "He just smiled at me. He held his arms out to me and beckoned with his fingers. I shook my head and said 'no'. He simply frowned and then walked away."

"Must have dreamt it," Mother said.

"Yes, must have!" agreed Lee.

His mother kissed him on his bandaged forehead and said "OK, love, I am off. I'll be back tomorrow. Oh! I nearly forgot, Maureen Reeves from the hairdressers called at the house to ask about you. Sends her regards." Lee smiled as his Mother left the ward.

Lee Penn had fancied Maureen Reeves since seeing her in a pub six months ago. She was with another bloke so he couldn't approach her. However, he did catch her covertly looking at him a few times. All he knew about Maureen was that she worked in a hairdressing salon on the High Street, the one his mother used. He also knew that she was very attractive with long, blonde, curly hair, that fell down to her shoulders and that she had a nice figure. It was Lee's plan to get his mother to ask a few discreet questions and find out if she was still seeing anyone.

*****

It wasn't long before Lee was back at work. He had worked as a clerk for Harrogate District Council since leaving Grammar School, aged sixteen, four years ago. He did not mind the work, although he found it repetitious. Still, he considered himself lucky. It was considered a safe job and there were not many of those about in 1971.

It was his practise to meet Greg in the Crossed Keys pub for a beer and a sandwich during his lunch hour. Greg Sanders was, at twenty three, a little older than Lee. He had longish, blonde hair that gave him a foppish look, befitting his job as an assistant librarian. He favoured tan coloured cord jackets, black slacks, shirt and tie. Not for him, the flared trousers that were in vogue. Although he dressed a little old-fashioned, he seemed to pull it off. He had quite an intellectual air about him and Lee had never heard him raise his voice.

"It's paid on," said Greg, from their usual table, as Lee entered the pub.
"Oh! Cheers!" replied Lee.
"How's the head?" said Greg, pointing to the scar on Lee's forehead.
"Fine, mate. I appreciate you coming to see me at the hospital."

Greg and Lee had a lot in common. They both lived with their mothers, both of whom were widows. They both liked books and films, and they could converse on almost anything. Greg's mother was Dutch, which was probably where he got his blonde hair from. "Hear you are seeing that lass from the hairdressers?" offered Greg, adjusting his Michael Caine-type glasses. "Maureen? Yes, been seeing her a few months now. Nice lass. Came to see me at the hospital. I think mum had something to do with it!"

Lee had never seen Greg with a woman. This surprised him because he was a good-looking lad. The story goes that he was once engaged and the lass ditched him for someone else. Apparently, he never got over it. Greg had never discussed it with him and he had never enquired.

"Do I hear wedding bells?" smiled Greg.

"I'll tell you what, mate, early days yet, but I wouldn't mind. I wouldn't mind at all!"

*****

Maureen and Lee had been going out together for three months and it was getting serious. Maureen was always playing the Carpenters' *For All We Know*. She reckoned it was their song. Lee had always got on fine with her parents, Joe and Betty Reeves, and they approved of him.

One Saturday, on Maureen's twentieth birthday, Joe offered them the loan of his car for a trip to Whitby. Lee had passed his test but had no car. The journey itself was a delight; driving Joe's Mini over the heather covered moorland and down the steep incline into the old fishing town of Whitby.

They enjoyed a pub lunch before climbing the 199 steps up to Whitby Abbey. The weather could not have been better as they made their way to the beach. The sea looked relevantly calm and Lee decided to go for a swim. He considered himself a strong swimmer and was soon breast-stroking away from the shore. All went well until he turned to head back to the beach. His legs cramped up and he suddenly found himself in a strong cross-current. He could see Maureen on the beach, standing up and gesturing to him to come in; whatever she was shouting was carried away on the wind. He was out of breath and the tide was not taking him out to sea, but along the shoreline; he couldn't get any nearer to the beach. His legs were no longer functioning and he was swallowing seawater.

This is the end, he thought, as a strange peace overcame him. He stopped struggling, looking up at the sky and the wheeling gulls. He closed his eyes and all he could hear was Karen Carpenter singing *For All We Know*.

*****

A sense of déjà vu overcame him, as he once again woke up in hospital. Only this time, there were two women giving him a hard time. "You were dead when they pulled you out of the sea. Do you know that?" Lee was unsure on how to answer that question. Maureen continued. "You were blue, bloody blue!"
"He was blue when he was born," interrupted his mother, "What they called a 'blue baby'… starved of oxygen…born dead, the midwife had to revive him."
Maureen and his mother then began an in depth conversation about blue babies, totally ignoring him. Lee was beginning to wonder if he was in some sort of private Hell. "Mum, I saw that man in black again!"
"What man in black?" demanded Maureen. Lee described what he had seen after the bike accident.

"So, what did he do this time?" said his mother, rolling her eyes.

"Same as last time really. But he seemed to be a bit more irritated this time when I refused his invitation to go with him." It even sounded silly to Lee.

"Maureen, for God's sake, marry the stupid bugger! You are his only hope!" said his mother, head in hands.

*****

In the three years they had been married, due partially to Lee receiving a promotion at work and Maureen buying a fifty percent interest in the hairdressers that she worked in, they were doing very well. They had a mortgage on a small bungalow and a second-hand Ford Cortina. The only dark cloud to hang over their marriage was that it was discovered that Maureen was unable to have children. For a short time, this put a strain on their marriage. But after test after test, they just had to come to terms with it. They lovingly decorated their bungalow and they even acquired a dog that Maureen spoilt rotten.

"We will have to do something about those curtains, love." said Maureen.

"Why, what's wrong with them?" replied Lee. What is it with women and curtains? he thought. That, and moving furniture around every other day…

"What's wrong with them…!?" she sighed, "Can't you see? They don't match the new colour we have on the walls."

"Oh! Yes, I can see it now. How could I have missed it?!" He nodded. It did occur to him to ask why they had not painted the walls to match the curtains in the first place. But he wisely held his council. Maureen gave him her 'Are you taking the piss?' look. For the record, he was!

"Right, love, promised Greg I would meet him for a pint," he said, kissing her. "Would you like anything bringing back?"

The Crossed Keys held the usual crowd of locals. Greetings were exchanged as Lee and Greg joined Old Albert and Tony Shawe at their table. Old Albert was what was known as a 'character'. He always wore a flat cap and smoked a pipe that never seemed to be lit. Dour by nature, he often surprised Lee with his acute insight and common sense. Tony Shawe was slight but strong, and could only be described as a 'street mechanic'. Nobody disputed Tony's skills as a mechanic. He could repair your car outside your home with only the minimum of tools and equipment, and all for a third of the price a garage would charge; of course, he did not have the overheads. Lee once asked Tony why he didn't rent one of the units on the Industrial Estate and set up shop there. Tony said that he didn't have the money, but Lee thought that the real reason was that he lacked the discipline to run a nine to five business. Tony wanted to work if and when it suited him, and it didn't suit him very often.

Greg began the conversation by asking if anyone had seen the documentary on television the night before about near death experiences. Nobody had. "What was it about then?" offered Old Albert.

"Well, as I mentioned, near death experiences: people who have technically died, but have been revived."

"Take Lee here!" continued Greg, "He has technically been dead twice!"

"What did tha' see, Lee?" asked Tony.

"Nothing really!" laughed Lee, then went on to describe the man in black he had seen on both occasions.

"That would be the Grim Reaper, Angel of Death, come for tha' soul," said Old Albert, knocking his pipe out.

"Well…" enquired Lee, "…if that was the Angel of Death, how come I am still here?"

"Yes," put in Tony, "The Grim Reaper doesn't ask thee nice to go wi' him. He just grabs hold of thee. Otherwise, nobody would die. They would just tell him to fuck off!"

Greg smiled and said, "I never thought I would say this, but Tony 'as a point!"

Tony basked in the praise.

"Out tomorrow night?" Greg asked Lee as they left the pub.

"Not sure, mate; tomorrow's Sunday. As you know, we are doing the bungalow up. I have a few chores to do, you know? Putting up shelves and curtain rods. If I can get done in time, I may be able to catch the last hour or so."

"OK, Lee. Maybe catch you tomorrow."

"Yeah, night, Greg."

"Night, Lee."

The next time Greg was to see him, he would be in a hospital bed.

*****

Sunday morning was to see Lee shouting out in pain and falling off the steps he was using, whilst drilling a hole in the wall to put up a shelf. Maureen, dropping her paint brush, ran to his side. "Are you alright? What happened?"

"I think I might have drilled into an electric cable?!" replied Lee, nursing his hand under his armpit. "We had better phone an electrician, if we can get one on a Sunday. Sorry, love."

After checking that he was OK, Maureen went to the phone. On her return, she found Lee apparently asleep on the settee. She tried to wake him. Unable to do so, she phoned for an ambulance. On his way to the hospital, Lee stopped breathing. The ambulance crew managed to revive him after just a few minutes, but it was a matter of concern for them. Lee was fine in the hospital and tried to reassure his mother and Maureen.

"They are naming this ward after you!" his mother said.
"Are they?" replied Lee. He wasn't joking…
"Christ…!" his mother moaned, "He has fried what little brains he had left. Maureen, please tell me that you have him insured?!"
"Up to the hilt!" Maureen nodded, "Up to the hilt!" Greg then entered the ward, and on seeing Lee, said, "Fancy seeing you here! Come on, they are letting you out. I will drive you all home."
After a cup of tea, Lee walked Greg back to his car. "I heard that you had stopped breathing for a time in the ambulance. Did you see our mysterious man in black

again?" queried Greg. "I did and he wasn't well pleased when I wouldn't go with him again… But whatever you do, don't tell Maureen!"

*****

Greg worked the Yale key into the lock and opened the door to his Mother's bungalow. "It's me, mum!" he shouted. A petite, blonde lady, probably in her late forties, greeted him. "Hello, mum, got your shopping. You have not met Lee, have you?" Lee held out his hand. "Hello, Mrs Sanders, nice to meet you."

"Oh! Please, Lee, call me Hetty!" she said in a voice that still held a trace of her Dutch ancestry. "Sit yourselves down boys and I will make us some tea." The lounge was spacious and very neat. Books on a multitude of subjects lined every available space and pictures of Dutch landscapes covered the walls. A rattle of cups heralded Hetty's presence as a large tray was set before them. "Help yourself to the cake, Lee. We, Dutch, love our cakes!" she said, pointing to the tray. "Greg was telling me about your near death experiences. Would you like to tell me about the figure in black you encountered?"

Lee, not for the first time, spoke of his meetings with the dark stranger. He explained how, on the first occasion, the man had been very kind. But on the following two occasions, he had become increasingly angry each time he had been denied. Hetty stroked her chin and looked worried. "I understand that you were born a 'blue baby'?"

"Well according to mum," confirmed Lee.

"So, basically, you have escaped death four times, if I include your birth?"

"If you put it like that, I suppose I have," agreed Lee.

Hetty continued, "In Holland, we call the man in black *Pietje De Dood*."

"The what dude?" frowned Lee.

"No!" said Hetty, looking uncomfortable, "*Pietje De Dood*: Peter the Death. He assists the spirit in its transition from this world to the next. In Holland, he is not seen as a figure to fear but as a friend, hence his pleasant demeanour. He wants to reassure the dying. This portrayal of the Grim Reaper with his cloaked skeletal body, scythe and hourglass is nonsense. That image was dreamt up by the renaissance painters during the Black Death. More tea?"

They chattered in general for a time, then to Greg's horror, Hetty got out the family photo albums. These showed black and white photos of a handsome man in uniform and a young Hetty. "Greg's father. We met during the War. Do you think that I have put on weight?"

As they were leaving, Hetty hugged Lee, looked him straight in the eye and said, "Lee, promise me you will be careful... Be very, very careful!"

*****

One Saturday morning, three weeks after Lee's visit to Greg's mother, the doorbell rang. This sent their terrier, Sam, into a yapping frenzy. "Shut up, Sam! I'll get it, love," said Lee, putting down his newspaper. On opening the door, there was no one there. He was just about to close the door when he noticed what looked like some kind of rolled up, medieval parchment on the doorstep.

"Who is it?" Maureen shouted from the kitchen.

"Nobody is there but someone left this," he said, undoing the black ribbon that secured the scroll.

"What is it?" she asked.

"Probably some kind of marketing gimmick," he said.

"Funny sort of marketing gimmick, written in a foreign language," she replied. She was right. Written on the parchment, in flowery copperplate, was this:

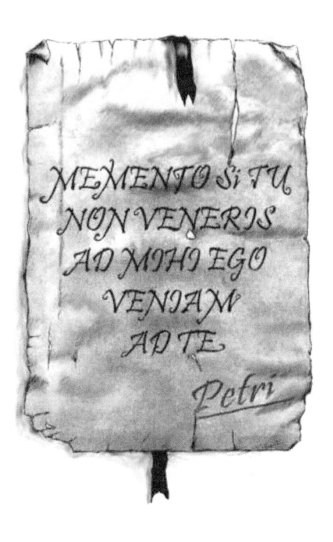

"MEMENTO SI TU NON VENERIS AD MIHI EGO VENIAM AD TE"

It was written in green ink and signed "PETRI".

"They have gone to a lot of trouble. It really looks old," he said. "I think the writing is Latin. I'll get Greg to have a look at it. He will know."

A month passed and Lee was lying down on the settee reading a book when the phone rang. "Oh! Hello, Greg. What's up?"

"Nothing, Lee. I just wanted to tell you that I showed that parchment that you gave me to a friend of mine at Leeds University. He seemed genuinely interested in it. He seems to think that it may be the real thing. However, it's not his field, so he wants to send it away for tests. I said I would have to ask you. What do you think?"

"Would it cost me anything for this test?" enquired Lee. "Oh! No, mate! I did ask… Actually, it could be worth a few bob. You never know!"
"Yeah, OK, Greg, let him send it for tests… If I get anything for it, you will be in for a cut!"
"Don't be daft. I don't want anything. How's Maureen?" asked Greg.
"She is at her mother's taking some curtains up on her sewing machine. I thought it was her calling!"
"OK, Lee. Let you go. Catch you later…take care."
"Yeah. Bye, Greg."

Lee closed the curtains against the night sky. It was getting late; Maureen should be home soon. He settled back on the settee with his book. Suddenly, without warning, the dog went berserk…howling and whining…running all over the bungalow! Lee had never seen him like that before. It scared the life out of him.

What he saw next really did scare the life out of him. Standing before him was Peter the Death. "But I am not ill?" thought Lee, "It must be a dream?!"

Peter the Death walked slowly towards him. He looked more sad than angry. Leaning over, he took Lee gently by the arms and he felt a swift lifting sensation as he left his body. It was as if a silk handkerchief had been whipped from the breast pocket of a jacket. He caught a glimpse of a star-studded sky as he quickly ascended and thought how beautiful it was. There was no fear, only a sense of wellbeing and belonging. He was going home. Maureen returned home to find Lee dead on the settee; a smile on his face.

The autopsy had shown that he died of a heart attack. It was three days before she could coax a cowering Sam out from under the bed.

*****

Maureen went to answer the door; three months had passed since Lee's funeral. Greg stood there. "Sorry to bother you, Maureen."

"Come in, you silly bugger!" she said, hugging him. Seated with a cup of tea, Greg explained that he wanted to return the scroll that had come back from the lab. "That silly thing?" she said, "I had forgotten all about it!"

"It's genuine, Maureen," he said, handing it over. "It's dated the fifteenth century, including the ribbon that bound it. The green ink had them baffled for a time; most ink from that period was black and made from carbon, gum and water. Apparently, this ink was made from vegetable matter, but it's from the same period: it's all authentic. It's a genuine parchment! Nobody would believe me when I told them you found it on the doorstep! Could be worth some money, Maureen, even if it's only as a curiosity piece."

"I'll tell you what, Greg - you were a good friend to Lee - he would want you to have it! Keep any money you get from it!" Maureen smiled and handed it back to him.

"No, I can't do that!" protested Greg.

"Please!" implored Maureen.

Thanking her, Greg got up to leave. At the door, Maureen said, "By the way, what did it say?"

Greg thumped his forehead. "Stupid of me, it's Latin as we thought: MEMENTO SI TU NON VENERIS AD MIHI EGO VENIAM AD TE. It means: *Remember, if you do not come to me, I will come to you.* It's signed 'Petri' which means 'Peter' in Latin. Does any of that mean anything to you?" Maureen thought for a moment. "No, not a thing!" she said. Walking to his car, Greg thought, "I know a Dutch lady that will understand it perfectly!"

Lives are not led but followed,
The shepherd and the lamb,
The piper and the man.

G.B. McClure

When the Green Leaves Fall

When green leaves fall
before the autumns call,
And old men cry before their final sigh,
Then what is this? I ask myself;
a kaleidoscope of things long past
and hopes and dreams beyond my grasp.

I see the sky but not the stars
and memories lie like mirrored shards.
A mop-haired child I used to know
is throwing snowballs in the snow.
He calls my name, remember me?
For I am you and you are me.

The days are short and winter calls;
shadows dancing on the walls;
sad ghosts of friends in dark corners lurk,
last seen at rest in a village kirk.
They avoid my eyes and turn away,
knowing I am them another day.

But still, I walk down old autumn's lane;
Sometimes sunshine, sometimes rain.
One day, the ferryman shall ask his fee,
I fear him not, for I cannot flee!
But why is this? I ask myself,
do green leaves fall before sad autumns call?

Footnote

When Green Leaves Fall was about the premature death of a good friend of mine. He was in his late fifties; not that young, but too young to die.

Is there a good age to die?

We had known each other from school, went down the mines together.

Then the Army, and later my thirst for travel took me away from home, and I did not see him for many years.

I learned of his death whilst attending a wedding and overhearing a casual remark…

The Hollow

What I am about to write is not a work of fiction. It is a true account of an event that happened to myself and a friend in the County of Norfolk, during the summer of 1966. This account is as accurate as my memory will allow, and there are no embellishments.

*****

My Battalion had just returned from a gruelling nine month campaign against Russian supported terrorist groups in the Saudi Arabian Port of Aden and the Radfan mountains. On returning to England in the summer of 1966, we were exhausted after long action against stubborn, and often elusive, foe.

After a short break, my Platoon was sent to Norfolk on a training exercise, basically acting as the enemy for another Regiment. We resented this as we felt we deserved a break from this type of activity. Also, we felt a bit funny firing blank rounds at other soldiers having just come back from the real thing.

We need not have worried. Our Platoon Commander and the NCOs felt the same way, and the exercise turned into a week long holiday. The sun shone every day, and at night, we slept under the stars. We had to put a bit of a show on to appease our acting enemy. So, we would occasionally put out a patrol and walk purposely into their badly staged ambushes. By doing this, we could 'surrender', then get back to lounging in the sun. They must have thought we were crap.

My story really begins on the last evening of the exercise. The following day we would be going back to our barracks in Tidsworth, Wiltshire. True to form, it was a warm, balmy evening, still plenty of daylight at 7pm. Feeling restless, I asked a corporal for the loan of his map. The map showed a small village about three miles from our camp. More interestingly, the village displayed the symbol for a church with a steeple: a circle with a cross on top. Now, my experience has shown me that where there is a church, there is a pub not too far away!

I approached a couple of mates, asking them if they wanted to accompany me to the village for a beer. They declined. I then approached Charlie. Now, Charlie was not a particular mate of mine, simply because we moved in different groups, but we were friends and I liked him. He somewhat reluctantly agreed. I asked permission from my officer to visit the village along with Charlie, and to my surprise, he agreed, on the condition that we were back in camp for 10pm. He knew me well enough to know I was not going there to take brass rubbings in the church…

The route to the village was simple: Follow the firebreak in a nearby conifer forest until we come to an open area; Once there, a gentle slope led down into a gully or hollow; At the other end of the hollow, a steeper slope led up to open grasslands with a path winding to the village.

Charlie was a Negro from the Blackboy Hill area of Bristol. (A place I would later come to know.) When amused, he had a very deep chuckle that everyone found delightful.

Charlie and I set off at a brisk pace and quickly arrived at the slope leading down to the hollow. Looking down, I was surprised to see what looked like a cluster of pebble dashed houses, bordering a dirt track; maybe six houses on each side of the track. These were not shown on the map and I concluded that they were forester's houses and the site was too small to be listed on the map.

Walking on the track between the houses, the first thing I noticed was the complete absence of noise: no music being played; no television; no radio; and, not a voice to be heard. Complete silence. I am not even sure if there was any birdsong. Even more eerily, there was not a soul in sight; not even a cat or a dog. Remember, this was a beautiful summers evening, about 7.30pm, with plenty of daylight left. I noticed Charlie was occupied with the houses on his right, whilst I was looking to my left. These houses were definitely in use, not derelict in any way.

As in any community, some of the houses and gardens were better maintained than others. Whilst some gardens bloomed with colour and had well kept lawns, others were overgrown with broken fences. I noticed in some gardens abandoned toys: a little, red, pedal car, similar to the one I had aged five in the early fifties; a dolls pram from the same era lay on its side...

But what I will never understand is why it took me so long to notice something which was so blatantly wrong - every single window of every single house was jet black. It looked as if all the glass had been painted black. No curtains and no reflections. Even some of the doors that had been left partly open showed nothing but a black void inside. Combined with the absence of life and noise, I cannot tell you how unnerving this was. It was as if the houses had lost their souls.

Compared to what happened next it seems irrelevant, but to me, it would eclipse what was to follow.

Reaching the top of the rise leading up from the hollow, we could see the village church steeple just a short walk away. What happened next defies all logic - but it happened!

It started as a faint rumble coming from the direction of the village. This rumbling sound increased alarmingly in volume as it rushed towards us at an incredible speed. I can only liken it to the sound of an express train bearing down on you. Within seconds, it had *WHOOSHED* over us, (Through us?) then just as quickly, it faded into silence over the hollow. We had both instinctively ducked. Immediately, in its wake, was a short blast of hot air; it was not unlike opening an oven door to check on a roasting joint and the heat jumping out at you.

We turned to look down onto the hollow. Nothing remained except a pleasant glade dotted with gorse and shrubs. Although the track remained, the houses had gone. No rubble or debris. They had just disappeared. A sense of relief flooded over me. Although I had not experienced a feeling of evil whilst walking through those haunted dwellings, I knew that they should not have been there in that time and space. I turned to Charlie's anguished face and he silenced me with a finger to his lips, before marching off. I cannot deny I was shaken and shocked by this recent event, but it seemed to have affected Charlie more than me - I was worried about him. Catching up with him, I put an arm round his shoulders as we completed our journey into the village.

The village was bathed in that golden light you get before day meets night. I was pleased to see that my instincts had not deserted me; there was a pub across from the church. On entering the pub, all the bar room chatter died out as the locals stared at us – well, two strangers in combat gear will do that!

I politely ordered two pints from the landlord who carried a military air about him. All soldiers can recognise this type. Officers who, upon leaving the service, still think that they are superior, especially when it comes to still serving soldiers. He placed the beers on the bar, along with my change, and said, "Make those the last ones, lads." I replied, not without some malice, "You got a problem with soldiers?" Charlie nudged me in the ribs and the landlord turned his back on me. Embarrassed and angry, I stood in the corner of the bar room with Charlie as the locals resumed their conversations. Draining our glasses, we placed them on the floor. If he wanted them, he could come and fetch them.

On leaving the pub, I voiced my disgust at the landlord's attitude to soldiers. Charlie, smiling at my naivetés, explained to me that the reason we were not made welcome was because he was black… I was speechless! That had never entered my mind! I argued that he was mistaken, but we both knew he was telling the truth.

The walk back to camp was uneventful. Approaching the hollow, I had half expected to see the houses standing there; that would have tipped me over the edge! I did scuff about a bit at the side of the track where the houses had stood, searching for some evidence that buildings had once stood there: footings; old bricks; broken glass; anything...but I found nothing.

Back in barracks, Charlie avoided me and an awkwardness developed between us. During our walk back from the village, I had quizzed him about what he had seen in the hollow. He flatly refused to discuss it with me, growing angry at times. I think he thought I would pursue it once back in barracks, though that was not my intension, but I could understand him thinking that.

Do not misunderstand me, he was always friendly towards me, but that awkwardness was always there - as if we shared a guilty secret. I think we were both relieved when he was moved to another Platoon.

*****

On writing, fifty four years have passed since the above events took place. Until recently, these memories have rarely surfaced. I thought that by writing about them I would find some clarification. I have not.

In retrospect, most of the things I witnessed in the hollow can be explained away, the exception being the windows. In fact, a lot of people have experienced far stranger things, myself included. Yet, it is the hollow that haunts me.

What happened on the rise overlooking the hollow cannot be explained.

I have come to accept that this was a paranormal event: houses don't just disappear. Yet, as strange as this episode was, it did not greatly trouble me, nor do I believe that it was the source of Charlie's distress. It has always been my belief that Charlie had seen something in the hollow that I had not - something that affected him badly.

I have never spoken about what I had seen that day and I am sure neither has Charlie.

The above narrative is true, but I take no offence to anyone who does not believe it.

Make of it what you will.

Footnote

Winter of 1967. I am walking through the streets of West Berlin. The city is mantled in snow and my greatcoat collar is pulled up against the cold. I study a bus stop timetable; I have a half hour wait for my bus.

Brushing the snow from my shoulders, I enter a bar. The bar room is empty with the exception of Charlie. He is sitting in a corner, nursing a beer. This makes for an awkward moment; I cannot just leave.

I take two beers over and join him at the table. After some small talk, an uneasy silence falls upon us. "Charlie…" I begin hesitantly, "…about the hollow…" He looked up from the table and met my gaze. The sadness in his brown eyes both overwhelmed and frightened me.

I drained my glass, adjusted my beret, and with a sad goodbye, left the bar. Walking back to the bus stop, I suddenly realised it was not the hollow that haunted me…it was Charlie.

Did You See the Soldier Fall?

Did you see the soldier fall?
Just before the bugle call,
crimson spreading on his chest,
in arid lands where eagles nest.

Did you see the soldier fall?
He will never see his daughter crawl.
His face a mask of stunned surprise;
a saddened look within his eyes.

Did you see the soldier fall?
Generals dancing at the Ball,
Politicians on the gravy train.
Could it be he died in vain?

Did you see the soldier fall?
His crying widow - proud and tall.
He went to save the Arab race;
the burning sun upon his face.

Did you see the soldier fall?

The Scarecrow

I had entered the wood three hours ago and had been following, what I took to be, an animal track; just a winding trail of beaten grass really. However, my compass showed me that it led in the general direction of the cathedral city of Wells. Wells was where I hoped to meet Marie; a girl I had met on an Israeli kibbutz the previous summer.

Hitching my pack, I wound my way through trees of beech, hazel, ash, oak and chestnut, amongst others, all dressed in their summer splendour and vying for the dappled sunlight that filtered down through their spreading branches. I continued at a leisurely pace as I was in no hurry. I was well equipped and planned to spend the night out in the open. Insects danced and droned about me in a symphony of sound and movement, as I passed beautiful glades filled with bluebells, wild thyme and common rockrose. Occasionally I spotted a clump of the rare and shy dog's mercury; its tiny, white flowers hiding amongst its broad, green leaves. Richard Dadd's paintings of fairies sprang to mind and I half expected to see a host of these woodland creatures dancing amongst the ferns and flowers.

Birdsong filled the branches with only the odd flash of colour betraying their presence. The heat, sounds and scents of this enchanted woodland made me feel drowsy and my pace slackened a little. A cuckoo called and was answered by the *rat-a-tat-tat* of a woodpecker. In the near distance, I could see the trees thinning out and a smear of blue sky.

On leaving the wood, I found myself looking down onto an expanse of rolling meadows, littered with wild flowers. I could not see any farm buildings, there was no sign of any kind of crops growing, nor was there any livestock that I could see; not even a cow was seen grazing these lush pastures. This suited me fine. The last thing I wanted was some grumpy farmer telling me to "Get off his land!"

Having left its zenith some hours before, the sun was falling towards late afternoon. I could see the towers of Wells cathedral in the distance under a blue sky marred only by a few wisps of mare's tail clouds.

A small clump of trees, which folded into a dip in the meadows, caught my eye, and I thought it may be a good place to camp. Jumping a small stream that hosted clumps of primroses and forget-me-not's, I headed down towards the trees. Startled rabbits scampered before me as they bobbed through dandelions, daisies and cowslips. The rich meadows of Somerset took on a golden glow and I could almost taste the cider.

Nearing my intended campsite, I discovered, that nestled amongst the trees, was what appeared to be a derelict cottage. I was just about to explore this ruin when I sensed a presence. That is when I saw him…half hidden by the trees, he stood, as if crucified on a small, wooden cross in the middle of a nearby meadow. Why would anyone put a scarecrow in an unploughed field with no crops?

Chiding myself for allowing him to startle me, I went to introduce myself. With a pumpkin for a head, he smiled down benignly at me, his mouth carved into a grin. He had a slit for a nose and two, large, round eyes that looked like bottomless pits. He wore old, corduroy trousers held up with a length of rope. An old jumper from which straw poked out through its many holes and a tattered jacket that completed the upper assembly. This was all crowned off with a battered felt hat which held in place a tumble of yellow straw hair. He had a sense of presence and dignity about him and I felt myself drawn to his deep black eyes. They seemed to pull me in and I felt like I was falling down a deep well.

Suddenly, his jacket started to undulate as if he had a heart and it had started to beat. Stunned, I stepped back. It was then that I noticed a cluster of little furry heads peeking out at me from behind the lapel of his jacket. It seemed that a family of field mice had made a home there.

As I left to explore the derelict cottage and prepare a campsite, I could feel the scarecrows' eyes on my back, but I sensed no malice there.

The cottage, or what was left of it, was hidden in a grove of alder trees. Nature, for the most part, had reclaimed most of the building, and the parts that remained were covered in honeysuckle and ivy. About a third of the stone structure remained standing, including the chimney stack. Most of the roof rafters had collapsed, and with the absence of tiles or slates, I was left to wonder if it had once been thatched. To the front of the cottage lay a small pond, heavily covered in pond weed. Parting the weed, I was able to see the dark, darting shapes of sticklebacks. Water beetles bussed up and down the green depths and swallows skimmed the surface for insects. A frog eyed me suspiciously through heavily blinking eyelids, before sinking below the surface. A small apple orchard, presently in blossom, completed the scene.

Clearing a space in a corner of the cottage that offered me the most protection, in the unlikely event of a change in the weather, I unrolled my sleeping bag and built a fire on the stone flagged floor. My old Army mess tin containing canned Irish stew was soon bubbling away and a packet of cream crackers was to be my bread substitute.

Later, mess tin cleaned and packed, I sat on my sleeping bag, back against the wall, drinking milkless tea from an enamel mug. A paperback edition of Laurie Lee's *Cider with Rosie* lay open on my lap. The light was still strong, but fading quickly, and I decided to keep the fire going, not for warmth but for light. Anyway, a fire is a good companion. Salvaging wood from a collapsed tool shed, I built up the fire, and lulled by the calling of wood pigeons, I began to dose. I was awoken by the sound of a strange shuffling sound. The daylight had gone and only the light from the fire held back the shadows.

Framed in what was once the doorway stood the scarecrow. Shuffling, on feet made of straw, he sat beside me. His Halloween pumpkin head with its fixed smile shone eerily in the firelight. Drawing his knees up under his chin, he produced a corncob pipe. Then, with twigged fingers, he picked up a glowing ember from the fire and dropped it into the bowl of his pipe. Pipe lit, he blew out tobacco smoke and turned towards me.

"You don't seem surprised to see me," he said, in a low voice with a soft Somerset burr.

"Well," I replied, "I was thinking of you when I fell asleep and now, I am dreaming of you."

"You think you are dreaming?" Had he an eyebrow, he would have raised it!

"Of course, I am dreaming!" I answered, "What else?"

"When does reality end and a dream start?" he questioned. "Maybe the dream is reality and reality is the dream?" he said, scratching his nose with the stem of his pipe. "Maybe life is death and death is life?" he continued.

"OK." I smiled, "It's not a dream. What can I do for you?"

"Oh, I just wanted a bit of company if you don't mind. I will go if you wish?"

"No need for that," I replied, "But be mindful of the fire. I am guessing that it would not take much for you to go up in flames!"

"The fire cannot harm me! If I was to catch fire, I would simply come back in another form; most likely a tree," he reflected.

"Who, or what, are you?" I didn't like the way this conversation was going.

"Well…" he said, pushing his hat to the back of his head, "I am an entity: a spirit, if you like. I have been about since the beginning of time. I have seen many things: herds of mammoths; knights in battle; marching columns of Roman soldiers… I am a watcher, a guardian of these ancient lands. There are others, of course. Some watch over rivers, lakes and streams. The Ancients called them sprites and they sometimes took on the form of a woman. Others guard the mountains in the guise of a rock or a rowan tree. The Ancients and the druids knew which rocks, stones and trees were inhabited by us and these places became sacred. Myself, and my ilk, watch over fields and pastures. I prefer the guise of a scarecrow, but sadly, they are rarely used in the present day. One day, I will fall and become one with the earth, just as man does. Then I will seek a tree to hold my spirit. I favour the cedar."

"My favourite tree," I said, almost to myself. A silence fell between us and, somewhere in the night, I heard the unmistakable bark of a fox.

"What are you reading?" he stabbed a twig finger towards my book.

"It's Laurie Lee's *Cider with Rosie.* For me, the best book ever to come out of Great Britain, and I mean, ever! Have you read it?" I said, without thinking.

"No, I am unable to read," he said softly. "What's it about?"

"It's about a young lad's rural upbringing in Gloucestershire in the early fifties. Laurie Lee, the author, would have understood everything you have told me tonight. Something puzzles me though," I said.

"Considering you have no crops to guard, and therefore are of no practical use, no offence intended, you seem very well put together?!"

"That's down to Old Granny Croft. She visits me when she can but she is very old now. She replaces the straw and ties me together. When needs be, my clothes are replaced. My hat is new. Do you like it?" he said, pointing to his hat.

"But why?" I asked, "Why does she do it?"

"Because these old country folk have the knowledge of the Ancients; not all of them, but there are still a few left. They know what and where we are. What rocks, stones and trees are sacred. That is why you will sometimes see trees with ribbons tied to them. They know where the sacred glades are in the woods where the guardians gather. They call them fairies. Granny Croft cares for me because she knows I am far more than a scarecrow: I am a guardian, an entity, a watcher." On saying this, he tapped out his pipe and stood, with some difficulty, to leave. "I thank you for the company," he said with great dignity.

"What is your name?" I said standing.

"Why 'Scarecrow', of course!" If his smile had not been fixed in place, I am sure he would have been smiling anyway.

"Yours?" he asked.

"Gordon." I replied.

"Well, Gordon, fare thee well!" and with that he scuffled towards the door.

"Wait!" I shouted, "I would like you to have this!" I placed my copy of *Cider with Rosie* into the inside pocket of his jacket. "I know that you can't read, but I have read this book many times and I just feel that you should have it. Consider it an offering if you like," I said, feeling just a little foolish.

"Thank you," he said, tipping his hat. "I will now let you continue with your dream…" Then the darkness swallowed him.

Morpheus released me from my sleep and I awoke to the sound of birdsong. Weak morning sunlight filtered down through the roofless rafters as I gathered my thoughts. Slowly, the previous night's dream came back to me and I remembered the scarecrows nocturnal visit in vivid detail. (This is unusual for me. Normally I can only remember a dream for a few minutes on waking. Then it slides back into my subconscious, like a whale sounding.)

Still pondering on my dream, I coaxed the dying embers of the fire back to life. Soon I had a brew bubbling away in my mess tin. I had arranged to meet Marie in the Rose and Crown pub in Wells at midday. A brisk pace would take me there with time to spare. Whilst drinking my tea, I noticed looking down on me from a rafter, a raven. It regarded me with a jaundiced eye before flying off. Tea drunk, I rolled up my sleeping bag and began packing my belongings. It was then I realised that I had lost my copy of *Cider with Rosie.* This puzzled me, but I could always replace it once in Wells.

Dousing the fire with pond water, I hoisted my pack. It was time to leave this strange but enchanted place. Making for what was once the door, my foot struck something on the floor and sent it skittering. Looking down, I saw a corncob pipe; it must have been there all along, I had just not noticed it. The memory of the scarecrow smoking a corncob pipe in my dream surfaced. Grinning, I thought I would give it to him as a going away present - I had planned to say goodbye to him anyway.

Approaching the scarecrow, I saw a raven perched on his shoulder. I found this quite ironic and stifled a laugh. I wondered if it was the same raven that I had seen earlier. I was almost upon him before the raven took flight.

"There you go, mate, you left this behind last night," I said, putting the pipe stem-first into his breast pocket. Turning to go, a great gust of wind sprang from nowhere, giving the effect that the scarecrow had momentary sprung to life. Turning on his crossed support, his arms and legs jumping as if in some crazy dance. Then, his jacket blew open, and there, in his inside pocket, nestled a paperback edition of *Cider with Rosie…*

Molly Malone

Bare footed, on cobbles, you haven't a care,
you stroll down old Grafton, defiant in stare,
you scorn all the gentry with a toss of your head,
but pity small children as they scramble for bread.

Dear Molly, my Molly, I watch from my door,
as rough men from the taverns your name they do call;
"A shilling for love," is what you declare.
As you take them to the Liffey, I can only despair.

I am but a poor man, no shilling have I,
but I love you, dear Molly, for you I would die.
I dare not approach you, for scorned I would be;
your laughter would soar up and float to the sea.

Taken by fever and hardship, poor Molly's long dead,
and I, now an old man, through old Dublin do tread.
But when the winds from the west and the city's asleep,
I go to the Liffey and for Molly I weep.

For there, in the moonlight, my Molly would sing,
"A shilling for love" and her laughter would ring,
"I told you, my poor man, I told you no lie,"
"For the likes of poor Molly, you never must cry."

Footnote

One night, I was sitting in a bar in Dublin, listening to a four-man folk group playing. During their break, they joined me at my table. (I think they fancied my girlfriend.) And we got to talking…

I asked them why nobody was playing any new material. All the folk groups were playing the same old songs - *Danny Boy,* etc. They agreed and explained that whilst they were able to compose music, they struggled with lyric writing.

At this point, deep in my cups, I offered to write something for them; pointing out that I did not know how to write lyrics as such, but I could write something in poem or prose form and they could 'doctor' it to fit their music. This was agreed and we arranged to meet the following night.

The next morning, regretting my promise, I staggered off to the library to research *Molly Malone*. This was pre-computer days.

*****

Why Molly Malone? Well, for a start, she was Irish, and according to my girlfriend, on the way back to the hotel the night before, I had had an in-depth conversation with Molly's statue in Grafton Street.

It is unknown whether Molly actually existed. There appears to have been a Molly Malone during the latter end of the 17th century. She was a shellfish seller by day and a prostitute by night. She died in her late twenties of fever.

I personally believe that Molly was an amalgamation of many young Irish women of that time, just trying to survive. I hope my poem treated her compassionately. God bless you, Molly.

*****

That night we met up with the group and I received four pints of Guinness for my services. They seemed pleased with my work. Never saw the group again, nor heard of a song named "Molly Malone" in the charts.

Oh well…!

The Clock Struck One

Norman and Betty Tyler were complete opposites. Yet they had shared fifteen reasonably happy years of marriage together.

Norman, an accountant, saw everything in black and white. As his profession suggests, he loved numbers. Numbers didn`t lie, they are what they are, unlike the written word. Some words, for example, are spelt the same but can have different meanings. These are known as homonyms. This is what you get when a language is made up from German, French, Latin and Norse, to name but a few.

No, numbers were true. They only have one meaning. If there is an error, it is a human error.

Norman loved nothing better than to see neat rows of figures that came to a logical conclusion. He wasn`t superstitious, he didn`t believe in fate or chance, everything ran on rails. In short, Norman was a descent, but methodical man, lacking in imagination.

In contrast Betty was gregarious, highly superstitious, and something of a scatter brain. Always reading her horoscope, she carried lucky charms by the score and often visited Mrs. Greene down the street to have her tea leaves read.

Betty was liked by everyone, but her forgetfulness could be annoying.

*****

"Did you get my razor blades, love?" said Norman, looking up from his newspaper as Betty stumbled through the door, laden with shopping.
"Razor blades?" she questioned. "Oh! Sorry Norman, I forgot them. I will go back out and get them."
"Don`t bother. I will call off and get them on my way to work. Why don`t you make a list?"

His irritation was obvious, and Betty`s chubby face crumpled in despair.
He often wondered why he had married her; they were so completely different. Yet, this was the very thing that had attracted him to her. She was a counter balance to his moody and solemn ways. He delighted in her "happy go lucky" ways and her optimistic view on life.

The thing with Betty was she really tried to get things right but seldom did. She tried very hard to please him. He loved her for that. She would attempt to cook fancy Italian or Indian dishes for him, but always forgot to add a vital ingredient and ruined the meal. He would pretend not to have noticed, but on realising her error, she would burst into tears. When it came to plain cooking, she was a good cook. Sometimes, she just tried too hard.

"Norman."

"What love?" he replied.

"Listen to this." she said, leafing through a book on star signs.

"Your star sign is Libra. It says that you are ruled by the planet Venus, your element is air, and your favourite colour is green."

"My favourite colour is blue." protested Norman, running his hand over his balding head.

Ignoring this, Betty went on. "It says your strengths are that you are co-operative, diplomatic, social, and fair minded. It goes on to say that your weaknesses are that you are indecisive, will carry a grudge, and are self-pitying. See, it`s true Norman. Do want to hear mine? Pisces?"

"If I must."

*****

The months pasted and they heralded in the New Year with a glass of sherry. "Well, I wonder what 1975 will bring us, Norman. My stars say it`s going to be a good year for me."

He wasn`t to know it yet but 1975 would be a very bad year for him.

"Cheers Ben." Norman raised his glass to his mate, Ben Austin.

"Cheers." returned Ben, lighting a cigarette.

They were seated at a table in the lounge of The Marquis of Granby. Both Norman and Ben were Knaresborough born, and had lived in this quiet Yorkshire town all their lives. Betty was from the neighbouring village of Kirk

Hammerton. It was a set routine Wednesdays, Fridays and Saturdays for them to meet up for a drink whilst their wives went to Harrogate to play bingo. Freda, Ben`s wife, would drive Betty there in her blue mini. Then, once the bingo was over, they would meet up with Norman and Ben back at the Granby for the last drink. They had been doing this for years.

Norman expressed his disgust at his recent pay rise. "I am forty years old, Ben. A trained accountant, and I am only getting £66 a week."

"You are doing better than me." replied Ben, gloomily "I am struggling to keep Freda`s old mini on the road." And so, the conversation went until the pub clock rested its hands on 10.30 pm.

"The girls will be in shortly." said Norman standing up. "Same again? Adele love, two pints please and take for the girls, will you?"

*****

Betty was crying because some character in Coronation Street had been killed off.

"For Christ's sake Betty, it`s not real, they are actors." Norman`s eyes rolled skywards.

"I know," she sobbed, " but she was a lovely lass."

"Never mind love. It's Blackpool in a couple of weeks. Don't forget your lucky bingo pen."

They had been going to Blackpool for their annual holidays for years. Same week in June, same guest house. They always stayed at the Parkfield Hotel on the South Shore. This was run by a Mrs O`Hara, an Irish lady that served excellent breakfasts. Norman wasn`t that keen on Blackpool. He found it too big and garish. He had fond memories of Cromer in Norfolk. He had gone there in his teens and found it quiet and relaxing, without all the big arcades and seaside rides. Still, Betty liked Blackpool, and it was easy to get to by train. He had never learnt how to drive.

*****

Two weeks later, they were strolling down central pier, walking off Mrs O`Hara`s massive breakfast. It was a sunny day, the sea was grey, and the gulls wheeled above them, buffeted by a strong breeze. Betty was like a big kid running from shop to shop.

"Hey, Norman look at this. That`s nice, isn`t it?" A wave of love for his wife suddenly swept over him, and it saddened him that at times he had acted boorishly towards her. She didn`t deserve it.

Taking her chubby little face in his hands, he kissed her on the forehead.

"Buy whatever you like love, whatever you like."

On the fifth day of their holiday, they were walking on the front when Betty let out a squeal of delight. "Oh! Look Norman, look!" She was pointing to a garish painting of a Romany woman looking into a crystal ball. The painting bore the legend "Roma Rose, fortunes told. £5 a reading". "Please Norman, let's go in. Please."

"Come on Betty, it's a load of rubbish. They are fraudsters."

"It's only a bit of fun Norman, pleeeease."

They entered the small, dimly lit kiosk to the strong smell of incense. The walls were draped in a heavy crimson material, and in the centre of the room stood a small round table covered in the same material. On the table stood a large crystal ball.

"Oh! Look." gasped Betty, pointing to the ball.

A curtain opened, and out stepped a woman in her early forties. She introduced herself as Roma Rose. Her appearance surprised Norman. He had expected some sort of old hag. But what he found was an attractive woman with long dark hair, wearing a loose floral top and a long black skirt. She was festooned with heavy gold earrings, necklaces, and bracelets.

'I am not surprised at a fiver a reading', thought Norman.

"Hello, mister, missus, you both like reading?" said Roma, in a heavy mid-European accent.

"No, I don't believe in that nonsense." replied Norman rudely.

Betty shot her husband a look and said. "Yes, please Roma, I would like a reading. That crystal ball must be centuries old."

"No, my dear." Roma laughed. "It is only about eighty years old. My mother, who also had the gift, left it to me. They are expensive because they are crystal, but anyone can buy one. You see missus, the power is not in the ball, but in the reader. The ball only helps the reader to focus his or her powers. So, sit down please, missus."

Betty could hardly contain her excitement as Roma huddled over the ball and looked deeply into it. As Norman looked on, the ball seemed to fill with a swirling blue vapour. He shook his head and looked again.

"Some bloody parlour trick" he muttered.

"What do you see?" gushed Betty.

"Patience please, missus."

Cupping her hands around the ball her stare intensified. Then Roma`s head suddenly jerked up and she looked straight at Norman.

Covering the ball with a cloth, she said, "Well missus, what I see is mixed. Before the year is out, you will come into a decent amount of money, but a loved one will die."

"Who will die?" said Betty, worry etched on her face.

"I cannot tell you because I do not know, missus." Roma said softly.

"It must be dad." said Betty, sobbing and holding her hand to her mouth. "He has cancer."

Norman exploded from his chair. "You bitch!" he snarled at Roma. "You have upset my wife with your lies. You are nothing but a charlatan, a fraud. I am going to report you to the council and get your licence revoked."

"I no lie." shouted Roma. "I only tell what I see in ball. If you want only pretty lies, you no come to Roma Rosie. Here, take back money and go." On saying this, she pushed the £5 note across the table to Norman.

"Look Roma, or whatever your name is, let's be sensible. All you have to do is admit to my wife that it was all a bit of nonsense and apologise and I will forget all about it. I will not go to the council, and you get to keep the money. What do you say?"

"No nonsense. I tell truth —" began Roma.

"You are a bloody LIAR!" interrupted Norman.

Roma's dark eyes flashed in anger. "You right Mister, I lie. I told missus I not know who die. I know who die. You die mister, you die. You want to know when? Sunday October 26th this year. At exactly 1.00am. When clock strikes one o'clock in the morning, that day you die."

*****

The remaining few days of the holiday where ruined, and it wasn't until they had been home for a couple of weeks that Norman finally managed to reassure Betty that Roma Rose's predication that he would die in October was rubbish.

"Don`t you see?" he reasoned. "She said it out of spite because I had slagged her off. She wanted us to worry about it."

Eventually, a tearful Betty agreed.

One Saturday night in September, Norman and Ben made their way to the bar in the Marquis of Granby. "Two pints please, Simon." Norman said to the landlord.

"Heard Man Utd thrashed Leeds last night." Norman said, trying unsuccessfully to hide a smirk.

"Have you ever considered drinking elsewhere?" scowled Simon.

"Tut-tut. Some people are so sensitive." a grinning Norman whispered to Ben.

"You know Alan and Trev, don`t you Ben?" asked Norman, joining the said mentioned at a table in the corner.

"Of course." replied Ben. "All right, lads?"

Alan and Trev acknowledged Ben`s greeting, then Alan said to Norman, "Don`t you dare say one word about last night's match."

"Alan." replied Norman, posing shock and throwing a wink towards Trev. "As if I would."

Trev, who was quietly doing the crossword, smiled and thought, 'here we go again'. Norman and Alan arguing about bloody football.

Taking a mouthful of beer, Norman, who was obviously in a mischievous mood, turned to Ben and said, "Trev`s got a preservation order out on him you know?"

"What the hell are you on about?" replied a puzzled Ben.

"Well," explained Norman, "All hippies are a protected species. You are not allowed to kill them by law."

"Christ." moaned Trev, shaking his head. "Where are Betty and Freda?"

"Bingo, where else?" said Ben. "Should be in soon."

"Good," muttered Alan. "We might manage to get a sensible conversation going at this table."

Right on cue the door flew open, and in burst Betty and Freda.

"Norman, Norman, you will not believe this. I have won £2000 on the bingo." said a jubilant Betty, thrusting a cheque into his hand. Then her face clouded in shock as she suddenly realised that the first of the two predications that Roma Rose had made had come true.

"Come on Betty think about it. How long have you been going to bingo? Five, six years? You have never had a big win until now. It had to happen sometime. It has nothing to do with Roma bloody Rose. So PLEASE, can we put this nonsense behind us once and for all?"

"Yes, I suppose you are right Norman." sighed Betty, frowning.

*****

Roma Rose had predicted Norman`s death to be on Sunday 26[TH] of October at exactly one o`clock in the morning.

Saturday 25th October saw Norman and Betty seated in their lounge reading. The walnut cased wall clock chimed midnight. If Roma was right, then Norman would be dead in an hour.

Both Norman and Betty pretended that they were not watching the minute hand on the clock slowly crawl over the Roman numerals towards one o'clock. At five minutes to one, the tension was unbearable, and Betty was the first to crack. She ran over to his chair and held his hand tightly, sobbing as she did so. The brass pendulum swung back and forth. Tick, tock, tick, tock, like a beating heart.

Norman found himself gripping the side of his chair with his free hand and when the clock chimed one, they both jumped, and Betty screamed. They waited a minute nothing happened. The waited some more. Still, nothing happened.

"See, I told you it was a load of bollocks." he said in a shaky voice. "Gypsy Roma! She couldn't predict what she was having for lunch."
Betty was both laughing and crying. "I will tell you what love, I have learned my lesson. I will never get involved with that stuff again."
The bedside clock showed 1.10am. "Have you got any indigestion tablets?" he asked his wife.
"Sorry love, a glass of milk might help. Would you like me to go downstairs and get you one?"

"It's okay I'll get it." he said, sliding his feet into his slippers.

A minute later Betty heard a massive thump and the sound of breaking glass. She found Norman slumped on the kitchen floor. One side of his face had collapsed.

*****

Sitting in the hospital corridor, she waited anxiously for news on Norman. They had told her that he had likely suffered a stroke. All that tension caused this, she thought. The trouble that bloody woman has caused.
Looking up, she noticed that the large electric clock on the wall showed 1. 55am. Thank God the hospital was near to their home. The ambulance had arrived in minutes.
A young doctor emerged from the ward. "Mrs. Tyler?" he asked. She knew straight away that something was wrong. "My name is Dr. Brookes. I am afraid your husband suffered a massive heart attack on his arrival. We tried to revive him, but he passed away at 1.00am. I am terribly sorry.
Glancing up at the clock, Betty looked puzzled. It read 2.15am.
"You mean he died at 2.00am, don't you? He was at home with me at 1.00am."
"I can assure you that he died at 1.00am exactly. I registered the time of death myself. We have to keep

accurate times for the records." he answered, wondering why it mattered to her.

She pointed to the wall clock.

"Oh! Now I understand." said Dr Brookes. "You see, today is Sunday the 26th October. At 2.00am the clocks went back an hour to Greenwich Mean Time. So, you see, the official time of death was 1.00am.

"Are you all right Mrs.Tyler? Mrs.Tyler?"

Tiger

Tiger eyes, in tiger gaze;
a sweeping look upon the stage.
Tiger hungry, tiger stare;
its prey at peace and unaware.

Tiger crouching, tiger spring;
the warning bells in heaven ring.
Tiger teeth and tiger claw;
henchmen knocking on the door.

Tiger running, tiger leap;
body falling at its feet.
Tiger gnashing with open maw:
tiger dripping; blooded; raw.

Tiger tearing, tiger eat;
crushing bone and ripping meat.
Tiger sleeping, tiger snore;
he heareth not the heavens roar.

Footnote

Tiger was triggered by a poster I saw in a shop window.

One summer's afternoon, I was walking to meet friends in Rose Cottage on the outskirts of Chichester. They had asked me to pick up a box of Cornflakes en route. Passing a shop, I noticed a large poster of a tiger in the window. This in turn got me thinking about Blake's poem *The Tyger* and then of tigers in general.

By the time I reached the cottage some fifteen minutes later, I had the completed poem scrawled out on the back of the cornflake packet.

I wish they were all that easy. A simple poem but I liked it for its energy. Alas, I was not too kind to poor tiger, only showing one facet of him.

About the Author and Photographs

The eldest of eight children, Gordon McClure was born in Wythenshawe, Manchester, in 1948.

Aged three, the family moved to Grimethorpe: a mining village in South Yorkshire.

A pupil at the local Secondary Modern School, he left aged fifteen, and worked underground in the village colliery for two years.

On leaving the mines, he enlisted and served six years in the Army. This was followed by many years of backpacking around Europe and the Middle East, before settling in Chichester, West Sussex.

He has two sons: Shaun and Glen - Shaun being the illustrator of this book.

The author lives in Knaresborough, North Yorkshire.

"A scattering of seeds..." - The McClure family

Back Row: Ian, Gordon (author), and Kevin.
Front Row: Alan, Bill (Dad), Steven, and Stewart.

Sisters: Sheena (now Cooper) Jean (now Allan), and
Sheena (Mum).

Printed in Great Britain
by Amazon

74307115R00119